Divine Apology

Divine Apology

The Discourse of Religious Image Restoration

BRETT A. MILLER

FOREWORD BY WILLIAM L. BENOIT

PRAEGER

Westport, Connecticut
London

Library of Congress Cataloging-in-Publication Data

Miller, Brett A., 1964–
    Divine apology : the discourse of religious image restoration / Brett A. Miller ;
foreword by William L. Benoit.
      p. cm.
    Includes bibliographical references and index.
    ISBN 0–275–97548–7 (alk. paper)
      1. Rhetoric—Religious aspects—Christianity—History. 2. Verbal self-defense—
Religious aspects—Christianity—History. I. Title.
BR115.R55M55   2002
273—dc21   2001058042

British Library Cataloguing in Publication Data is available.

Library of Congress Catalog Card Number: 2001058042
ISBN: 0–275–97548–7

First published in 2002

Praeger Publishers, 88 Post Road West, Westport, CT 06881
An imprint of Greenwood Publishing Group, Inc.
www.praeger.com

Printed in the United States of America

The paper used in this book complies with the
Permanent Paper Standard issued by the National
Information Standards Organization (Z39.48–1984).

10 9 8 7 6 5 4 3 2 1

Contents

Part III: Interpretations

Foreword

Image repair discourse, or *apologia*, has been a recognized fruitful area for rhetorical criticism for decades. Essays in the 1950s by Baskerville (1952) and Jackson (1956) may constitute the earliest such studies. Rosenfeld's Nixon/Truman analogy (1968) was followed by one of the most famous studies in this area by Ware and Linkugel (1973). The majority of work on *apologia* (as *Divine Apology*'s review demonstrates) has focused on political and corporate image repair, with relatively few studies of religious *apologia*. *Divine Apology* is an important contribution to the literature and should redress the existing imbalance. Although a few book chapters and articles cover this topic, this is the first extended work in this area.

Apart from the importance and past neglect of the topic it takes up, *Divine Apology* is a solid, well-written rhetorical criticism. First, the texts selected represent a very useful balance between historic and contemporary *apologia*. Moreover, *Divine Apology* critically analyzes a wide range of apologies: individual rhetors and groups as well as rhetors defending against a variety of accusations. The scope of this study makes it an important contribution to our understanding of religious image repair.

Second, Professor Miller has done a fine job of critically analyzing these artifacts. He begins (à la Ryan, 1982) with a careful consideration of the context and accusations that prompted these image repair efforts. When he turns to critical analysis, he actively *engages* the text, helping his analysis come alive for readers with appropriate excerpts and keen insights. When he takes up the task of evaluating these discourses, he judges their appropriateness and then seeks evidence, where available, to confirm his assessments.

In many ways the heart of the book comes in the final two chapters, in which *Divine Apology* teases out implications for religious rhetoric and for image repair discourse. Insights are offered for rhetorical theory generally, for *apologia* specifically, and for religious discourse. Students and scholars in any of these areas would find this book very rewarding. Professor Miller has written a fine book, an important contribution to our understanding of religious *apologia*.

William L. Benoit
University of Missouri–Columbia

Acknowledgments

It would be completely inappropriate if I did not begin by establishing my indebtedness to William Benoit. His mentoring, guidance, and encouragement were invaluable to me as I pursued this project. Pamela Benoit also read early drafts of this manuscript and provided important theoretical and structural support. Critical commentary by Michael Kramer and Michael Porter helped make this a better book. Paul Johnson was extremely helpful in causing me to question my perspectives and to stretch beyond the comfortable. I thank Joseph Blaney for setting the bar high and supporting me with candor and good humor through the research and writing process. My editor, Suzanne Staszak-Silva, the production staff at Greenwood, and the anonymous reviewers for my manuscript provided some insightful guidance. I owe a great debt to Stephanie Schierholz for her assistance in preparing the final manuscript. I also wish to thank numerous teachers and colleagues, including Holt Spicer, Donal Stanton, John Sisco, James Sneegas, Gary McGee, Penni Pier, and Bob Derryberry, who assisted and influenced me in one way or another. Finally I thank my friends and family, especially Betsy, Cassidy, and Carsen, for their patience and grace.

Introduction:
Saving Faith, Saving Face

With the possible exception of modern science and scientific enterprises, no subject or endeavor has influenced the shaping of culture or the content of human discourse more significantly than religion. Even for individuals who claim to be untouched by faith or spiritual conviction, the effects of religious values and linguistic performance are inescapable. It is arguable that Christianity, in particular, with its nearly two billion professing adherents, has presided over the mind and communicative behavior of Western society for nearly two millennia. While it would be inaccurate to suggest that Western culture is completely "Christianized," it would be appropriate to note that a Christian *Weltanschauung*, or worldview, is at work strongly influencing morality, politics, education, rhetoric, and many other facets of public and private life. Even those institutions and activities that are opposed to—or even consciously antagonistic of—faith-based perspectives, often exist in a dialogical relationship with various expressions of Christianity. The consequence is that a tremendous amount of our communicative behavior is influenced by the culture-structuring impact of this religious ethos.

In much the same way that religious faith impacts society, the rhetoric of image restoration pervades public discourse. Fisher (1970) maintains that communication is fundamentally based on motives that consider image as a central issue. Benoit (1995a) extends this position when he argues that discourse designed to purify image is one of the most recurrent features of human communication behavior. We all feel a powerful need to build and maintain favorable reputations. From the schoolyard, to the workplace, to the White House, image restoration discourse is a ubiquitous phenomenon.

With a dominating social force such as Christianity operating within a rhetorical milieu that regularly involves the defense of image, it is inevitable that Christian rhetors will face the need to present *apologia*, or persuasive defense, in response to *kategoria*, or persuasive attack. As an enormous ideological presence in the world, Christendom has played host to a tremendous number of conflicts physical, mental, and spiritual in their variety. From early persecutions of believers and medieval inquisitions to modern political and doctrinal squabbles, Christian rhetoric has been fraught with persuasive attack and defense. And, while it is important to examine how faith influences the strategies of Christian rhetors, it is with equal or greater interest that I consider how rhetorical actions reveal the nature of faith.

Therefore, my aim is to investigate image restoration rhetoric as it concerns and is performed by religious rhetors. The enormous impact of Christianity on the world and the pervasiveness of face-saving rhetoric suggest that each might be understood more fully if we examine the nature of faith-based *apologia*. Moreover, researchers (see Blaney & Benoit, 1997; Sullivan, 1998a) have called for a wider application of *apologia*, specifically image restoration theory, beyond the range of political, corporate, and celebrity apologies. The specific focus on Christian *apologia* should contribute to the growing interest among rhetorical scholars (Berry, 1998; Heisey, 1998; Hobbs, 1998; Klope, 1998; Reagles, 1998; Gring, 1998; Sullivan, 1998b) in an emerging theory of Christian discourse. Perhaps, then, the focus of this project will serve to enhance our understanding of faith and rhetoric.

APOLOGIA AND APOLOGETICS

Before proceeding, it is important to draw a precise distinction between *apologia* and what has been known in Christian scholarship as apologetics (see Carnell, 1956; Dulles, 1971; Ramm, 1961; Sproul, Gerstner, & Lindsley, 1984). Sullivan (1998a) clarifies the difference when he argues that *apologia* is *rhetorical* discourse that addresses specific cases and specific audiences; apologetics is *dialectical* discourse that addresses general questions and universal audiences. For instance, if a church leader argues that a personal, powerful being called God created the world, he/she is engaging in apologetics. If a teachers' union attacks a state senator's public image because he/she believes in a literal Genesis account of creation, the discourse may become *apologia*. Certainly, there will be occasions when the genres will blend, but the rhetorical-dialectical bifurcation provides a means of distinguishing the two and dividing ground.

Christian *Apologia*

To further illustrate the nature of Christian *apologia*, and to demonstrate the dearth of such research, consider these studies that examine the apologies of Jesus, Francis Schaeffer, and Charles Colson. Blaney and Benoit (1997) evaluated Jesus' persuasive defense of himself as recorded in the *Gospel of John*. In response to such accusations as blasphemy, violation of religious law, and demon possession, Jesus primarily responded by transcending the issues or simply denying the alleged offenses. While he failed in the immediate situation and was ultimately executed by crucifixion, Blaney and Benoit argued that Jesus' defense was successful in a broader historical context. They further suggested that since religious discourse often presumes "that earthly concerns are ephemeral, that the body is less important than the soul, that there are higher purposes, or that a wonderful reward awaits us in the afterlife" (p. 30), then transcendence is a particularly appropriate strategy for rhetors defending theological doctrines.

Sullivan (1998a) analyzed conservative Christian author Francis Schaeffer's apology in *Pollution and the Death of Man*. Two scientists had written separate articles attacking Christianity for fostering environmental irresponsibility. Each scientist argued that ecological policies are an outgrowth of religious belief, and since Christianity fosters the anthropocentric idea that nature exists solely for the service of humans, Western technological advancement has been valued more than the preservation of natural resources. In response, Schaeffer attacked these accusations as illogical and manipulative, shifted the blame to the more extreme fundamentalist Christian groups, but confessed and apologized for Christians' unwillingness to speak out against the abuses of capitalism. Sullivan found Schaeffer's argument pedagogically useful, but not particularly compelling as a coherent *apologia*.

McLennan (1996) took up the case of Charles Colson, the former special counsel to President Nixon, who was imprisoned for his part in the Watergate coverup. Colson converted to Christianity and wrote a book called *Born Again*. McLennan characterized the book as an attempt to revitalize Colson's public image, helping Americans "cleanse themselves of their collective guilt about Watergate" (p. 12). Colson identified himself with the biblical conversion of the Apostle Paul. He differentiated his new self from the old self. He confessed and sought forgiveness, following the archetypes of ritual redemption. Since Colson "exercised the appropriate stages to fulfill his audience's appetite for transformation of this sort" (p. 12), McLennan assessed Colson's *apologia* as successful.

Such studies of Christian *apologia* are mixed in their usefulness. Alone, they are somewhat helpful in understanding the image repair strategies available to particular religious rhetors; however, as a group they lack a consistent standard for analysis and explanation.

IMAGE RESTORATION DISCOURSE

In his seminal work, *Accounts, Excuses, and Apologies* (1995a), William Benoit presents a theory of image restoration discourse that provides a comprehensive and unified approach to the analysis of *apologia*. Integrating rhetorical perspectives (Burke, 1970; Rosenfield, 1968; Ryan, 1982; Ware & Linkugel, 1973) with social science approaches (Goffman, 1967; Scott & Lyman, 1968),[1] Benoit develops an exhaustive typology for image restoration strategies.

Arguing that communication is driven by goals and motives, Benoit contends that the need for image purification is a fundamental human drive. However, for rhetors to feel compelled to defend themselves, an audience must believe that an act has been committed that they (the audience) consider offensive; and, the accused must believe that the salient audience considers him/her responsible for the offensive act. In both cases, perception is important. Benoit reasons, "Before people are prompted to restore their image, they must believe the audience holds them responsible (for an act they think the audience believes is offensive)" (1995a, p. 72). This position is refined (see Benoit & Dorries, 1996; Benoit & Wells, 1998) by showing the

Table 1.1
Dimensions of Persuasive Attack

Increasing Perceived Responsibility for an Act
  The accused committed the act before.
  The accused planned the act.
  The accused knew the likely consequences of the act.
  The accused benefited from the act.

Increasing Perceived Offensiveness of an Act
  The audience was affected.
  The extent of the damage was significant.
  The negative effects persisted.
  The act was a case of inconsistency (hypocrisy).
  The victims were innocent/helpless.
  The accused had some obligation to protect the victims.

---

accused is responsible for the act because the accused committed the act previously, the act was premeditated, the accused knew the likely consequences of the act, or the accused benefited from the act. Offensiveness is developed by showing that the damage from the act was extensive, the negative effects of the act were ongoing, the act affected the salient audience, the act was a result of inconsistency or hypocrisy, the victims were helpless, or the accused was obligated to protect the victims. The dimensions of a persuasive attack are summarized in Table 1.1. With these assumptions in place it is possible to describe the various strategies for repairing and maintaining a favorable reputation, or face.

Benoit (1995a) creates a typology for image repair strategies by formulating five general categories: denial, evasion of responsibility, reducing the offensiveness of the act, corrective action, and mortification, which are further subdivided. Denials can take the form of simple refusals to accept culpability, or in effect denying the accusations by blaming another party. Responsibility can be evaded by claiming to be provoked, by claiming defeasibility ("It was out of my control"), claiming that it was an accident, or claiming to have had good intentions. The accused can reduce the offensiveness of the act by bolstering their reputation, minimizing the severity of the untoward act, differentiating the act ("I wasn't *stealing*, I was *borrowing*."), transcending the context ("There's a much bigger issue here

Table 1.2
Image Restoration Strategies

Denial
    simple denial
    shifting the blame

Evading Responsibility
    provocation
    defeasibility
    accident
    good intentions

Reducing Offensiveness
    bolstering
    minimization
    differentiation
    transcendence
    attacking accuser
    compensation

Corrective Action

Mortification

---

that we are missing."), or attacking the accusers. The accused can also offer to take corrective action. Finally, the accused can engage in mortification by admitting to wrongdoing and seeking forgiveness. These strategies are summarized in Table 1.2.

This typology of strategies, couched within a comprehensive theory of self-defense rhetoric, provides a consistent and unified method for rhetorical analysis. A great wealth of *apologia* research[2] has been conducted exclusive of Benoit's theory; and, while I generally would not question the scholarship of these studies—many of them have added a great deal to our understanding of the theory and practice of rhetoric—as a collection of works they provide an incomplete perspective on the nature of apology. Moreover, they do not work in concert to incrementally enhance our understanding of the rhetorical contexts (political speech, corporate advocacy, celebrity image repair, etc.) in which they occur. Image restoration theory contributes more to the study of *apologia* as a communication genre. It also works to more precisely define differences in rhetorical practices. However, even with the abundance of recent research using image restoration theory, there has been little discussion of how the accumulated strategies begin to tell us something about the classes of rhetoric within which they are practiced. Therefore, it is important to briefly examine how image restoration strategies reveal the nature of political, corporate, and celebrity discourse.

For instance, Benoit and his colleagues have compiled a good amount of research on political rhetoric from which some informed commentary can come. Utilizing an early form of image restoration theory, Benoit, Gullifor, and Panici (1991) studied Reagan's discourse during the Iran-Contra affair. They found that he used conflicting strategies by first denying that he ever traded arms for hostages, then claiming that the exchange was made with good intentions. Ultimately, Reagan accepted responsibility for the act and promised corrective action. This confused strategy and failure to accept the blame early was deemed a failure in strategy.

In a 1970 speech, announcing a U.S. offensive into Cambodia, Nixon provided an "anticipatory image restoration" (Benoit, 1995a, p. 143), because he was not responding to a specific accusation. Recognizing that his actions would be controversial, Nixon first bolstered his position by aligning himself with past warring presidents. He differentiated "offensive" from "invasion," so as to annex the policy onto previous, ongoing actions. Nixon also transcended the issue by claiming that his actions were directed toward ending the war. Benoit found this example of preemptive *apologia* to be less than effective, suggesting that if Nixon had relied more on bolstering and transcendence, without attempting the differentiation, he may have been more successful.

In another study of political *apologia*, Benoit and Nill (1998a) considered Clarence Thomas' defensive statements before the Senate Judiciary Committee. Thomas denied Anita Hill's sexual harassment charges with a simple, categorical repudiation of the attacks. He bolstered his image by recalling his record and reporting that he had been responsible in his treatment of Hill, as well as by casting himself as a victim in the confirmation process. Thomas also identified the senators conducting the hearings as accusers and attacked them as being racists. Benoit and Nill determined that Thomas' *apologia* was well-constructed and instrumental in providing the means and the motivation for the committee to confirm him.

After receiving widespread criticism after a controversial book deal, former Speaker of the House Newt Gingrich defended himself through a combination of denial, claiming good intentions, bolstering, attacking his accusers, and promising corrective action. Kennedy and Benoit (1997) found that Gingrich's *apologia* was not successful, because he was internally inconsistent in his strategies. He essentially claimed to have done nothing wrong, then promised that he would correct his wrongdoing; furthermore, external evaluation showed that the public attacks did not cease.

A number of studies have considered the apologies that have come from the Clinton administration. Benoit and Wells (1998) examined the program of defense designed to repair the images of Bill and Hillary Clinton in the midst of the 1994 Whitewater scandal. The Clintons and their numerous surrogates denied any wrongdoing. They bolstered the images of the Clintons by referring to the president's policy achievements and the first lady's legal and healthcare reform efforts. They all transcended the issue of Whitewater by calling their audience to redirect their attention to the problems of the nation. Benoit and Wells argued that Bill Clinton's defense was the most well-conceived and effective, with Hillary Clinton's *apologia* appearing more defensive and less persuasive.

Benoit (1999) further examined Clinton's rhetoric when he evaluated the president's *apologia* in the Whitewater affair, the Paula Jones lawsuit, and the Monica Lewinsky scandal. The main strategies Clinton employed were denial, attacking accusers, transcendence, and mortification. While there were some significant contradictions in these tactical choices, and his political opponents were not persuaded, Benoit found that Clinton's discourse was generally effective with the voting public.

Blaney and Benoit (2001) found a similar tendency in Clinton's rhetoric when they examined his apologies during the Lewinsky scandal. He used a number of strategies, but the general trend that emerged was a volley of denials that were offered until they were no longer plausible in the face of the evidence. Then, he established a "culture of transcendence" when he successfully convinced the public that his misdeeds, even when eventually admitted, had little to do with the substantial interests of the government.

What we discover in these studies is that all five primary strategies of image restoration were available and useful to political apologists, nearly all of whom chose to employ multiple strategies rather than gamble on a single strategy. As a class, they seem to use transcendence and attacks against their accusers with some regularity. The use of complementary strategies, such as Reagan's eventual mortification and corrective action, appears to be more successful than contradictory tactics, like the use of denial and transcendence by numerous Watergate defenders. Also, contrary to claims of some (see Kruse 1981b) that defenses of policy are not appropriately studied as *apologia*,[3] in these studies defenses of policies and character issues did not seem to operate with any significant difference. This would suggest that, indeed, defenses of policy can function as *apologia*. Finally, it seems that political figures who failed to accept blame in the face of overwhelming evidence of their culpability were generally less successful than those who accepted at least partial responsibility.

Corporate image repair discourse appears to be similar to political rhetoric, but with some notable differences. The presence of consumer response and legal liabilities seem to shape the way companies construct defenses. These perceived restrictions create limitations and confusion in developing a defensive program. An example is Exxon's defense. The highly publicized *apologia* in the wake of the 1989 *Valdez* oil spill involved a denial that shifted the blame to Captain Hazelwood, the state of Alaska, and the Coast Guard. The company minimized the scope of the ecological damage. Exxon also bolstered its image and promised corrective action in an open letter. While the blame-shifting and promise of corrective action were marginally successful, Benoit (1995a) claimed that, overall, the strategies were terribly ineffective. Perhaps the pressures of the marketplace and threats of legal action made the company slow to accept the blame.

Sears offered a similarly ineffective apology in 1992. The giant retailer was accused of automotive repair fraud by the California Department of Consumer Affairs. Providing no supporting evidence, Sears denied any wrongdoing. The company differentiated terms by saying things like instances of "fraud" were really "mistakes." The company attempted a variety of other strategies involving good intentions, bolstering, and minimization. Sears attacked its accusers as being politically motivated; and it finally promised corrective action by changing its policies. Sears' image repair efforts were ineffective because the company failed to engage in mortification when facing obvious and overwhelming evidence of guilt (Benoit, 1995b).

Other cases of corporate apologies that were incomplete, or mixed in their effectiveness, include Dow Corning, which first denied the harm of silicone breast implants, then later accepted responsibility and took steps to prevent further problems (Brinson & Benoit, 1996). After an airline accident, USAir bolstered its image, denied a history of safety violations, then finally moved toward corrective action by undergoing a voluntary safety audit (Benoit & Czerwinski, 1997).

Following the deaths of customers afflicted with *Escherichia coli*, the Jack in the Box company denied responsibility and bolstered its image. It claimed defeasibility by suggesting that the grill heat standards were unclear, and offered corrective action in new cooking heat standards. The company offered compensation to the victims, but minimized the situation by accepting only partial responsibility (Sellnow & Ulmer, 1995). In such cases of mixed success there is usually a shift in apology approach that is too little too late.

Successful cases include AT&T's defense of itself in 1991 when the telecommunications company suffered a significant disruption of service to its East Coast customers in 1991, resulting in millions of people left without service and a large amount of air traffic on the ground. While the company's immediate response was to shift the blame to its workers, the strategy was quickly changed to involve an open letter published in newspapers all over the country. The letter included mortification in the form of an unambiguous apology from the chairman, promises of corrective action, and bolstering the image of AT&T as a company of high reputation (Benoit & Brinson, 1994).

Texaco and Schwan Sales Enterprises also performed examples of relatively effective defenses. Texaco was accused of racism in 1996 after company executives were caught on tape using bigoted language. After first bolstering the quality of the company and shifting the blame to a few "bad apples" in management, the company publicly said it was sorry and launched a zero-tolerance discrimination policy (Brinson & Benoit, 1999). In an even more successful rhetorical move, Schwan's limited its response to mortification and corrective action following a 1994 outbreak of salmonella in its ice cream products. The company recalled the products and offered free medical treatment. Since its products are delivered (and recalls were collected) by route drivers, each driver was able to provide a face-to-face apology. Moreover, the company announced a change in its truck fleet that would prevent further such problems. Sellnow, Ulmer, and Snider (1998) found the Schwan's strategy to be a model for corporate crisis communication. In these successful scenarios, the companies risked possible litigation by admitting guilt, but managed to reduce public accusations and negative media attention through honest acceptance of responsibility and meaningful corrective action.

Like political apology, the image restoration discourse of corporations utilizes the same range of strategies, but with different emphasis. There is clearly less interest in attacking accusers or engaging in transcendent rhetoric in corporate defenses. While denials and bolstering are as common, corrective action is far more prevalent. Even though the risk of litigation arises, the effective corporate apologists recognize the purifying power of mortification more than their political counterparts.

Celebrity *apologia* operates in much the same way as political and corporate defenses, with the primary exception that the content of the apologies is likely to focus more on character issues rather than policy defenses. In a well-conceived, but poorly delivered case, Tonya Harding sought to repair her image after accusations that she was involved in the attack on her Olympic skating rival, Nancy Kerrigan. Harding denied involvement, bolstered her character, attacked her ex-husband and her bodyguard as her prime accusers, and claimed defeasibility because the situation was out of her control (Benoit & Hanczor, 1994).

In two similar and successful defenses, Oliver Stone and representatives for the *Murphy Brown* television show used denial, bolstering, and counterattacks. In response to criticisms about the conspiracy theories promoted in the movie *JFK*, Stone initially denied any inaccuracies, then went on to bolster his sources and strongly attack his accusers in the media (Benoit & Nill, 1998b). After accusations by Vice President Dan Quayle that the show promoted single motherhood, the producers of *Murphy Brown* denied his charges, attacked Quayle, and bolstered the Murphy Brown character as a caring mother (Benoit & Anderson, 1996).

Benoit (1997) examined actor Hugh Grant's defense of himself after he was arrested for soliciting a prostitute. Grant used the strategies of mortification, bolstering, attacking accusers, and denial; but, he failed to make his repentance sufficiently clear and contrite.

In a rather unique celebrity *apologia*, Queen Elizabeth defended the royal family when it was accused in 1997 of not displaying sufficient grief after the tragic death of Princess Diana. Benoit and Brinson (1999) found that the Queen denied the accusations, bolstered the image of the royals, claimed defeasibility in excusing the royal family, and used transcendence in calling Britons to come together before the world.

As with political and corporate *apologia*, celebrity defenses make frequent use of denials and bolstering. Unlike political cases, however, celebrities are less likely to transcend the issue to some higher social good. Queen Elizabeth is an exception, but is perhaps a hybrid example of political and celebrity apology, since she is at least marginally concerned with the matters of state. Also, celebrities were more likely than corporate apologists to use attacks against their accusers, and less likely to promise corrective action. This could be attributed to the lack of a clearly defined consumer base and the focus being more on character defense than policy defense.

In the cases of *apologia* considered, there appear to be no other defensive strategies available to the rhetors, other than those outlined by Benoit. Thus, the typology of image restoration theory seems to be complete. All the strategies are available to apologists, and to students and scholars alike. Therefore, image restoration theory provides a standard of analysis that provides for thorough, consistent evaluation, and the compiling of cumulative rhetorical artifacts.

This is important when we are interested in saying something about image restoration discourse as a speech genre, and when we hope to comment on such genres of public communication as political, corporate, celebrity, and religious rhetoric. By establishing how different speech genres behave within the context of image restoration, we can deepen our understanding of different rhetorics. For instance, in the area of religion—particularly Christianity—where there exists no real sense of rhetorical identity, the use of image restoration theory can serve to define tropes and commonplaces within the discourse. Over time, such consistent evaluation promises to move image restoration theory beyond a primarily descriptive function to the point of suggesting prescriptive rhetorical moves. The weight of cumulative findings can begin to press a template of sorts for future apologists. It is with these aims in mind that we turn to our objects of analysis.

A brief guide to how I plan to proceed is in order. First, some assumptions. The analysis in this book will be conducted with the assumption that, for the most part, the rhetorical artifacts represent the speakers' rationally constructed positions. This may not always be the case, but since it is not within the scope of this project to plumb the depths of the rhetors' psychological motives or true intentions, I submit that it is sufficient to treat their messages as reflective of what they meant to communicate. Just like persuasive defenses are not motivated by actual events, but perceived events, so is this analysis based on perceived intent, rather than objectively identified motives and events. I also assume that the more important the rhetorical situation, and the more time involved in the construction of the message, the more rational the rhetorical choices are likely to be. A conversational utterance is far less likely to embody a rational perspective than a speech or written document that has received a tremendous amount of forethought. Since most of these examples of discourse deal with matters of significant gravity, and they are written documents or prepared speeches, it seems reasonable to assume that they represent conscious, rational choices. In particular, religious rhetors are likely very aware of the antecedents in their respective genres (Jamieson, 1973), or the previous discourse in their fields, and seek to maintain some type of consistency with their spiritual lineage. Therefore, it is not unreasonable to assume that their image restoration discourse will be constructed with a significant amount of attention to this lineage and the consequences of the rhetoric.

My next assumption is that the widely available, translated texts of the historical rhetoric are sufficient for evaluation. Where it is appropriate, notations will be made concerning the availability and reliability of texts. It is not my intention to engage in historical-critical analyses of texts. It is, however, my intention to examine the functions and effects of those texts as they are received by salient audiences. For instance, it is not ultimately important to this project to determine whether Paul wrote the letter to the Galatians. Whether it is an authentic document, or a cultural construction of early Christian writers, it has served as an exemplar of Christian *apologia*, and is perceived (by salient audiences) to be a somewhat authoritative document. To eliminate or diminish a text from this study because of its indeterminate authorship is to neglect the importance of historical and contemporary audiences far removed from the original context, who have no access to the original discourse. The focus of this study is not on evaluating the *authors*, but on evaluating the *discourse*.

I assume that a case of image restoration is best understood when taken as a speech set. Each of the six instances of *apologia* will be described in relation to the prompting *kategoria*, or attack. In the cases where there is no specific attacking text available, or when the defense is preemptive in nature, the attack will be described as it is taken to have been perceived by the apologist(s).

The cases under consideration are all taken to represent a protestant lineage in Christian discourse. That is not to say that each is Protestant in some official capacity. Clearly some of these apologists represent, on some level, a heritage that is Catholic in nature; however, the themes brought out by the rhetors—such as salvation by grace alone, evangelicalism, individualism, and biblical authority—are issues that have become, perhaps, more representative of a protestant tradition that does not necessarily consider the historical church or church authority for its validation.

In order to explore fully the nature and scope of "protestantic" *apologia*, the following chapters examine the rhetoric of historical and contemporary Christian apologists as they face charges brought against their beliefs and behaviors. The historical-contemporary comparison is intended to illuminate any enduring characteristics in Christian discourse. Furthermore, by examining the rhetorical form of *apologia* from ancient through current practice, it is possible to more fully understand the scope of change or unity in the genre.

In chapter one, I consider the apology of the Apostle Paul contained in the *Letter to the Church at Galatia*. Paul's apologies were primarily directed to fellow believers, both Jewish and non-Jewish converts, in defense against charges by agitators and rival teachers that he was corrupting the faith by encouraging converts to ignore Jewish law and accept salvation through grace. He confronted perceived accusations that he was not an authentic apostle for the followers of Christ. This chapter explores the possibility that a defense of a belief, or policy, can function as a defense of image. In this case, as in most religious contexts, the image of the rhetor is inextricably bound to the beliefs professed.

Chapter two considers the defenses of Justin Martyr during the post-apostolic second century. Attacks against Christians from outside the church were on the increase. Responding to such charges as cannibalism, incest, treason, atheism, and the general degradation of the Greco-Roman world, church leaders such as Ignatius, Tatian, Tertullian, and Justin began to publish answers to the accusations of civil authorities and contemporary intellectuals. Justin's *Apologies* are a unique form of image restoration rhetoric in that they blend a defense of policy and character; moreover, when these defenses were delivered, the apologist almost certainly was aware that his words would likely cost him his life.

The final historical case, in chapter three, examines Martin Luther's defense of himself and his doctrinal beliefs at the onset of the Protestant Reformation. In particular, my analysis focuses on Luther's apology before the Diet of Worms in 1521, where he faced charges of heresy, with the possible penalty of excommunication. The event has not only had significant implications historically and religiously; I propose that Luther's apology begins to shape the parameters of modern protestantic rhetoric.

With the first of the contemporary cases I move well into the twentieth century. Chapter four investigates the apologies of the colorful televangelist, Jimmy Swaggart. In a situation far removed in time and circumstance from his historical predecessors, Swaggart faced the need to account for himself in the midst of a public sex scandal. After campaigning for years against various brands of sins and sinners, Swaggart was accused of having adulterous relations with a prostitute. His program of defense is unique in how he used the language of Pentecostal faith to expunge himself from guilt and restore his damaged image.

In chapter five, I consider the defensive rhetoric that has emerged from the contentious struggle over the historical Jesus. The Jesus Seminar, which began in 1985 as a collection of scholars aiming to determine and publicize the authentic words and deeds of Jesus through scientific inquiry and media exposure, published numerous books and held public events that called into question the faith-based beliefs of many Christians. Interpreting the organized publicity of the Jesus Seminar as orchestrated attacks against orthodox, evangelical Christianity, opponents to the Seminar began to publish responses designed to restore the image of traditional Christian views of Jesus. The apologies considered in the chapter represent the unique behavior of religious *apologia* when opposing views are separated by a deep epistemological divide.

For several years through the 1990s the Southern Baptist Convention (SBC) passed controversial proclamations, drawing criticisms from various quarters. In chapter six, I examine the Southern Baptist responses to public attacks after the Convention determined that the proper role for women in the family was a posture of submission to their husbands. While it is difficult to ascertain an official message from the denomination—with "the priesthood of the believer" and a measure of commitment to individual autonomy—the apologies of various high-profile SBC representatives are tracked as they are reported by the media. As one of the most protestantic of the major Christian denominations, this image restoration discourse is an important exemplar of how *apologia* within a protestant lineage performs.

The final two chapters are designed to take the analyses of these historical and contemporary cases and apply them to the evolving theories of religious rhetoric and image repair. In addition to fleshing out the theoretical textures of image restoration discourse, I discuss how these defensive moves in religious communication assist us in defining the nature of Christian rhetoric.

NOTES

1. See Chapter 3 in Benoit (1995a) for an exhaustive treatment of social scientific research on accounts.

2. A substantial amount of research on political *apologia* (Benoit, 1982; Blair, 1984; Brock, 1988; Brummett, 1975; Butler, 1972; Collins & Clark, 1992; Gold, 1978; Haapanen, 1988; Harrell, Ware, & Linkugel, 1975; Heisey, 1988; Huxman & Linkugel, 1988; Jensen, 1988; Kahl, 1984; Katula, 1975; Ling, 1970; Rosenfield, 1968; Ryan, 1982, 1988; Vartabedian, 1985), corporate *apologia* (Foss, 1984; Hearit, 1995, 1996, 1997; Ice, 1991; Sellnow, Ulmer, & Snider, 1998; Tyler, 1997), and celebrity *apologia* (Kruse, 1981a; Nelson, 1984) has been conducted exclusive of Benoit's theory.

3. Kruse (1981b) argues that *apologia* only concerns defenses of character, not defenses of policy. This position severely limits the apologetic situation, especially where religious discourse is concerned. This study considers defenses of policy as *apologia* , because the policies—beliefs and doctrines—of religious believers are not as easily separated from their identity as corporate, professional, or even political policies may be in other cases.

Part I

The Historical Apologists

1

Paul's Apostolic Apology in the Epistle to the Galatians

Saul of Tarsus, a Jewish rabbi and Roman citizen, was a prominent persecutor of early Christians in the first century A.D., until he experienced a dramatic conversion while traveling to Damascus (Acts 9:1–19).[1] He changed his name to Paul and became a prolific preacher, prominent apostle, and "next to Jesus, the most important and enigmatic figure in the initial stages of Christianity" (Meeks, 1972, p. xi). His numerous missionary journeys, public rhetoric, and influential epistles made Paul "the great conduit through which Jewish concepts and stories and patterns of thought came to the Gentile world" (Wilson, 1997, p. 28). This Jewish enforcer, who had once martyred followers of Jesus, became the most notable figure of early Christianity.

While writings and actions attributed to Paul—which comprise nearly a third of the New Testament—are replete with sermons, hymns, theological treatises, apologetics, and personal reflections, perhaps as interesting as any of his rhetoric is his defense of the image of Christianity, and subsequently himself. One particularly noteworthy case of such a defense is found in his Letter to the Church at Galatia. Accepted and canonized as part of the New Testament,[2]

Paul's defense has, for centuries, served as a model for Christian *apologia* inside and outside the community of believers.

While hundreds of volumes have been written about the historicity, philosophy, and theology of Paul, few studies have considered Paul's discourse *as rhetoric*.[3] The most substantial message-centered analyses of Pauline rhetoric were done by Kennedy (1980, 1984). He observed that Paul implemented some classical rhetorical devices when he wrote that the letter to the Galatians "can be analyzed in terms of an 'apology' of the classical sort" (1980, p. 130). Most notably, however, Kennedy characterized Pauline rhetoric as a rejection of classical philosophy and rhetoric in its paradoxical claim to gain strength through weakness and wisdom through foolishness (see I Corinthians 1:18–27). However, with the single exception of Betz's (1979) theological commentary, Paul's discourse has not been considered as *apologia*. Certainly, no rhetorical study has analyzed the precise image restoration strategies he used.

In Galatians, Paul delivers an *apologia* designed to defend theological premises and to purify his image among the early Christian believers. While this letter resembles the dialectic of apologetics, in that there are universal arguments that could be applied to general audiences, on the whole this document represents a rhetorical defense aimed at a specific audience situated in a specific context. Through a blending of character and policy defenses, Paul creates an *apologia* that is wide in scope.

The text of Galatians is a case of worlds colliding. Paul represented a doctrine of grace, maintaining that first-century Christian believers could have complete faith in what God had done for them; conversely, his opponents represented a doctrine of works, supporting the idea that believers should base a portion of their faith on what they did for God (Witherington, 1998). Phillips (1955) characterizes the Galatian problem as a conflict between "believing and achieving" (p. 9). Wilson (1997) widens the argument to a conflict between Jewish Christians who sought to preserve a nationalistic exclusivity in their religious culture and Paul's desire to universalize Christianity. Howard (1979) supports this claim when he writes, "What we get in Galatians is a glimpse into that moment of Christian history when steps were taken to expand the borders of the church for the incorporation of all nations" (p. 45). In either case, there is a fundamentally important epistemic conflict at stake: Was the Christian gospel to be understood as an emancipatory message, broad in its appeal, or was it to be viewed as a mere annexation in Jewish tradition, exclusive in its membership? While it is not the function of this chapter to provide a theological or historical examination of these issues, it is within the purview of the study to explore this conflict in the context of Paul's rhetorical defense.

THE ATTACKS AGAINST PAUL

The source(s) for the accusations against Paul are not entirely clear. Jewett (1971) offers an explanation of Paul's opposition in Galatia when he argues that the Zealot movement during the middle of the first century A.D. was determined to rid Israel of all Gentiles (non-Jews); therefore, the Zealots opposed what they perceived to be Gentile sympathizers like Paul:

> My hypothesis therefore is that Jewish Christians in Judea were stimulated by Zealotic pressure into a nomistic campaign among their fellow Christians in the late forties and fifties. Their goal was to avert the suspicion that they were in communion with lawless Gentiles. It appears that the Judean Christians convinced themselves that circumcision of Gentile Christians would thwart Zealot reprisals. (p. 205)

Others have claimed that Paul's opponents were Gentile Judaizers and spiritual radicals—"pneumatics" (Ropes, 1929), Jewish mystery cult syncretists (Crownfield, 1945), or Jewish Christian gnostics (Schmithals, 1972). However the most widely held view is that they were Jewish Christian judaizers (see Howard, 1979, pp. 1–19) who were pressuring the Galatians to observe the precepts of Jewish law. Whoever they were, they are never clearly identified in Paul's discourse.

Sometime near A.D. 53–54, Paul apparently spent some time teaching predominantly Greeks (Gentiles) in the region of Galatia (Meeks, 1972). After his departure, these Jewish Christian judaizers encountered the same believers and commented on the failure of the new converts to be circumcised. The Galatians responded that Paul had been with them and had made no mention of the need for circumcision. To these judaizers, circumcision was the *sine qua non* for spiritual redemption; therefore, they opposed Paul in Galatia, claiming that he had watered down his message—failing to require adherence to Jewish law—in order to win the confidence of the Galatians.

The charges are not clearly stated in the letter. In fact, it is unclear if formal, public accusations were made at all. Nevertheless, Paul responds to what he clearly believes to be accusations from fellow believers. It is important to remember here that a rhetor need only to believe that he/she has performed an act that is perceived as offensive by an audience (Benoit, 1995a). Suspicions and concerns in the mind of the rhetor may operate the same as an overt attack. So, even though there is no documented *kategoria*, Paul's letter is an answer to perceived attacks.

The consensus among historical and contemporary commentators (see Bruce, 1982; Luther, 1535/1949) is that Paul wrote the letter in response to two primary accusations. First, his message of grace and his lack of emphasis on religious law were weakening, or perverting, the gospel. Second, his authority as an authentic apostle was illegitimate, since he was seen as having removed many requirements of Jewish law in order to convert Greeks and non-Jewish people.

These charges serve as a persuasive attack, motivating a defensive posture, by casting Paul as responsible and offensive in his actions. He was considered responsible in that he knew the likely consequences of his actions; he was viewed as offensive primarily because he appeared to be inconsistent with his professed beliefs. He was born a Jew, had studied rabbinical law, was converted to the Christian sect within Judaism, and was commissioned to teach the gospel by the apostles in Jerusalem who practiced circumcision and observed Jewish laws and customs (Witherington, 1998); so, he was seen as "betraying his ancestral heritage" (Bruce, 1982, p. 26) when he failed to require obedience to religious law. He clearly would have understood the impact of his teaching, and what his perceived obligations would have been.

The charges of his opponents amounted to a "personal attack upon Paul which he bitterly resents and to which he here replies in a good deal of heat" (Ropes, 1929, p. 12). He is motivated to defend himself as an authentic apostle to the Christian faith, and he is motivated to defend his doctrine of grace.

A CRITICAL ANALYSIS OF PAUL'S APOLOGY

Various scholars (Bruce, 1982; Howard, 1979; Kennedy, 1984) divide Galatians into three primary sections: the autobiographical or personal apologetic section (chapters 1–2), the theological or dogma section (chapters 3–4), and the ethical or practical application section (chapters 5–6). However, image restoration strategies are used throughout the text. Paul employs the strategies of bolstering, attacking accusers, and transcendence.

Bolstering

Paul uses bolstering to reposition himself as a credible source, to reestablish his ethos with the Christian church in Galatia, thereby answering the concerns about his authenticity as an apostle. Each example of bolstering is designed to reduce the offensiveness of his teachings.

In the first instance of bolstering, Paul makes the critical claim that his message is the result of divine appointment when he begins his salutation, "Paul, an apostle—sent not from men nor by man, but by Jesus Christ and God the Father, who raised him from the dead—and all the brothers with me, to the churches in Galatia" (1:1–2).[4] By making this claim, Paul is doing more than promoting himself as the mouthpiece of God; he is distinguishing himself as independent from the Jerusalem apostles, but fully apostolic nonetheless. Furthermore, in his autobiographical narrative (1:13–24) that follows, he details his history as a former persecutor of the Christian church who had subsequently been "set apart" and "called" by God, and who "did not consult any man" in his ministry. This instance of bolstering serves the purpose of diminishing the offensiveness of his actions by elevating the character of his authority. As a speaker in possession of God's authority, he bolsters his image as an authoritative apostle in the eyes of the Galatians.

In his second instance of bolstering, Paul demonstrates that he is credible because he had received support from the "pillar apostles" in Jerusalem, and that he has intentions of carrying out the typical work of an apostle:

> James, Peter, and John, those reputed to be pillars, gave me and Barnabas the right hand of fellowship when they recognized the grace given me. They agreed that we should go to the Gentiles, and they to the Jews. All they asked was that we should continue to remember the poor, the very thing I was eager to do. (2:9–10)

In essence, Paul is aligning himself with the images and personalities that had achieved widespread acceptance in the churches of the region; moreover, he establishes that he had received approval from those leaders. Therefore, his image as an authentic apostle to the Christian churches was further bolstered.

In his third instance of bolstering, Paul seeks to reduce his offensiveness among the Galatians and cultivate an intimacy with them by writing, "I plead with you, brothers, become like me, for I became like you" (4:12). Bruce (1982) interprets this as Paul saying that he wishes the Galatians would show the same friendship and confidence in him as he has shown them. He bolsters his image by reminding his audience that he has done them no wrong and that he is their friend.

The final case of bolstering comes near the end of the letter when he closes, "Finally, let no one cause me trouble, for I bear on my body the marks of Jesus. The grace of our Lord Jesus Christ be with your spirit, brothers. Amen" (6:17–18). Bruce (1982) catalogs various perspectives on what Paul meant by the "marks" he bore. His physical marks could have been from a reported stoning he had received for his beliefs, a body-marking in the form of the letter X (the first letter of the Greek form of "Christ") that he might have received at his baptism, a blindness he suffered as a result of the brilliant light present during his conversion experience, or some other sort of religious brand. Regardless of the actual marking, his rhetorical claim here is that he was to be trusted because he had been marked. He had been physically stigmatized (Wilson, 1997), for the sake of the faith.

Perhaps what is most interesting about this general strategy is that it follows a chronological sequence of focus. First, Paul associates himself with God: a universal being and presence. Second, he associates himself with the pillar apostles: an earth-bound representation of God's authority. Third, he associates himself with the Galatians: a more localized community of God's presence. Finally, he presents the image of his person: the most specific agent of God's presence. It is as though this strategy is designed to take the audience through a series of associative steps from God to the speaker.

These tactics function to bolster Paul's image and to specifically answer the perceived charges against his apostolic authority. In these passages Paul claims divine appointment and guidance, demonstrates his acceptance within the ranks of the church leadership, establishes his history of friendship with the Galatians, and reminds his audience of his personal commitment to the faith. This strategy promotes Paul's ethos, and works to reduce the offensiveness of his actions.

Attack Accusers

At numerous points in the letter, Paul chooses to attack his accusers as a strategy for creating distinctions. He seems to be distinguishing himself from his opponents by casting them as malevolent interlocutors; moreover, he creates a separation between their legalistic practice of circumcision and his message of grace and freedom. He accomplishes this through attacks directed at beliefs, or policies, as well as attacks directed at the character of his opponents.

First, in the attacks against his opponents' doctrines, Paul treats their teachings as a corruption of the truth, worthy of severe condemnation:

> I am astonished that you are so quickly deserting the one who called you by the grace of Christ and are turning to a different gospel—which is really no gospel at all. Evidently some people are throwing you into confusion and are trying to pervert the gospel of Christ. (1:6–7)

He completely rejects the requirement of circumcision and the teaching of strict observance of Jewish law. He follows this condemnation with a harsh curse, "If anybody is preaching to you a gospel other than what you accepted, let him be eternally condemned!" (1:9). So, early in the letter, Paul delivers a severe denunciation of his opponents and their teachings.

Later in the letter, Paul issues a softer attack that might be better characterized as a rebuke when he writes:

> You foolish Galatians! Who has bewitched you? Before your very eyes Jesus Christ was clearly portrayed as crucified. I would like to learn just one thing from you: Did you receive the Spirit by observing the law, or by believing what you heard? Are you so foolish? After beginning with the Spirit, are you now trying to attain your goal by human effort? Have you suffered so much for nothing—if it really was for nothing? (3:1–4)

It is important to note that this attack is primarily directed at Galatian believers who have adopted the teachings of Paul's opponents. Perhaps the inclusion of Galatian church members in this attack causes Paul to treat their offense with a rebuke for misfeasance instead of the curse reserved for the willful malfeasance of his primary detractors.

The final policy attack aimed at the legalistic doctrines of the judaizers is framed as a warning for believers. "You who are trying to be justified by the law have been alienated from Christ; you have fallen away from grace" (5:4). By representing justification through Jewish law as an offensive belief, Paul seeks to restore the image of his doctrine of justification through grace.

The second form of attack Paul makes against his accusers is aimed at the character of his opponents. He represents them as immoral and consumed with their own agendas when he writes:

> Those people are zealous to win you over, but for no good. What they want is to alienate you from us, so that you may be zealous for them. It is fine to be zealous, provided the purpose is good, and to be so always and not just when I am with you. (4:17–18)

He continues these claims, and further accuses them of hypocrisy, when he states:

> Those who want to make a good impression outwardly are trying to compel you to be circumcised. The only reason they do this is to avoid being persecuted for the cross of Christ. Not even those who are circumcised obey the law, yet they want you to be circumcised that they may boast about your flesh. (6:12–13)

So, Paul works to reduce the offensiveness of his discourse by casting his accusers as selfish and inconsistent.

Beyond these attacks on his opponents' actions, Paul delivers further scathing character attacks concerning the diabolical nature of his accusers and the consequences of their offenses. He claims they are ungodly when he writes, "You were running a good race. Who cut in on you and kept you from obeying the truth? That kind of persuasion does not come from the one who calls you" (5:7–8). He warns of punishment for the responsible parties, "The one who is throwing you into confusion will pay the penalty, whoever he may be" (5:10). And in a statement of bitter sarcasm, Paul lashes out at his opponents who teach the requirement of circumcision, "As for those agitators, I wish they would go the whole way and emasculate themselves!" (5:12). Paul makes it very clear that his opponents are to be viewed as evil people that deserve judgment and self-mutilation.

In summary, Paul does engage in vigorous attacks against his accusers. These policy and character attacks serve to promote the image of Paul's teachings by juxtaposing his theology of grace and his honorable character—promoted through his bolstering rhetoric—with the legalism and the selfish motives of his Judaizer opponents.

Transcendence

Paul also attempts to restore his image by placing the issues in a larger, more important context. In his use of transcendence, Paul abandons references to his character as an apostle and positions everything in reference to larger faith issues. Essentially, Paul uses transcendence through three primary rhetorical strategies.

First, he argues for an immutable truth that is bigger than his particular situation or agenda. Near the beginning of the letter he claims that his message is about something much more significant than the promotion of his reputation when he writes, "If I were still trying to please men, I would not be a servant of Christ" (1:10). As a way of clarifying this transcendent appeal, he explains:

> I want you to know, brothers, that the gospel I preached is not something that man made up. I did not receive it from any man, nor was I taught it; rather, I received it by revelation from Jesus Christ. (1:11–12)

Far from being a case of defeasibility, where the events of the situation are simply out of the rhetor's control, this appeal to a higher truth, or authority, portrays the issue as much broader and more significant than a personality conflict between Paul and his opponents. He focuses on the importance of this ultimate condition when he states, "I assure you before God that what I am writing you is no lie" (1:20). Later he asks, "Have I now become your enemy by telling you the truth?" (4:16). And he further defines his truth as unique from the truth of his opponents by writing, "But by faith we eagerly await through the Spirit the righteousness for which we hope. For in Christ Jesus neither circumcision nor uncircumcision has any value. The only thing that counts is faith expressing itself through love" (5:5–6). These appeals to ultimate truth are part of an attempt to transcend the particular issues and reduce the offensiveness of Paul's discourse.

In the second transcendence approach, Paul argues for a unifying of believers, thus diverting attention away from the perceived offensiveness of his actions and focusing on the advancement of the faith. He begins by justifying his teachings as important in the effort to proselytize the Greeks and non-Jews. "For God, who was at work in the ministry of Peter as an apostle to the Jews, was also at work in my ministry as an apostle to the Gentiles" (2:8). However, he goes on later to argue that the ultimate result is a unification of all people in the faith:

> You are all sons of God through faith in Christ Jesus, for all of you who were baptized into Christ have clothed yourselves with Christ.

There is neither Jew nor Greek, slave nor free, male nor female, for you are all one in Christ Jesus. If you belong to Christ, then you are Abraham's seed and heirs according to the promise. (3:26–29)

These passages function to direct attention away from the charges against Paul by refocusing attention on the universality of the Christian message.

Third, he maintains that the real battle is not between his detractors and him; it is between the archetypes of good and evil. In this form of transcendence, Paul dramatizes his message of faith and grace as the good, and he characterizes the message of his opponents as evil. He begins this distinction when he states:

We who are Jews by birth and not "Gentile sinners" know that a man is not justified by observing the law, but by faith in Jesus Christ. So we, too, have put our faith in Christ Jesus that we may be justified by faith in Christ and not by observing the law, because by observing the law no one will be justified. (2:15–16)

He strengthens the distinction and heightens the drama when he says, "So you are no longer a slave, but a son; and since you are a son, God has made you also an heir" (4:7). He further develops this metaphor (4:21–30) depicting those who live under the traditional Jewish law as the children of a slave woman who will never share in the father's inheritance. He describes those who live under grace as the children of a free woman, calling them, "children of promise" (4:28). By stating, "Therefore, brothers, we are not children of the slave woman, but of the free woman" (4:31), he completes this particular argument.

By positioning his actions against the landscape of religious destiny, Paul transcends what he perceives to be accusations against his character and policies. With one of his final points in the letter, he engages in the most conspicuous form of transcendence: "Neither circumcision nor uncircumcision means anything; what counts is a new creation. Peace and mercy to all who follow this rule, even to the Israel of God" (6:15–16). With this claim, Paul transfers the attention away from the accusations against him, and instead directs his audience to the more expansive concerns of theological truth.

This analysis shows Paul using the image restoration strategies of bolstering, attack accusers, and transcendence. Next it is important to assess the effectiveness of his discourse.

EVALUATION OF PAUL'S DISCOURSE

This assessment of Paul's letter to the Galatians will begin by evaluating the appropriateness of the various strategies. After appraising each rhetorical choice for its aptness, I consult various sources for evidence of external effectiveness of the letter.

It should first be noted that Paul never denies, evades responsibility, engages in corrective action, or mortification. All of his strategies are designed to reduce the offensiveness of his perceived actions and to rebuild the image of his character and policies.

Paul's use of bolstering was a fitting tactic for addressing the character issues. For him to continue as an authentic apostle to the Christian churches, he had to reestablish his credibility as a religious authority. By claiming divine appointment, he answers perceived accusations that his particular brand of theology was simply a Pauline construction. Perhaps anticipating that his claim of heavenly enlightenment would alienate him from the existing Christian leadership, he appropriately associates himself with the authority and approval of the Jerusalem apostles. Next, he asserts his friendship with the Galatians. And his final bolstering effort is to draw attention to his suffering and *stigmata* that were a result of his personal faith journey. The implicit structure in Paul's bolstering strategies appears to be an appropriate argument designed to lead his audience through a series of rational steps to recognize his credibility. This structural design and the specific strategies themselves were suitably chosen.

Paul's attacks against his accusers seem to be an appropriate response to the accusations he perceived as being directed at him. By launching these counterattacks, Paul drew a bright line of distinction between the opposing doctrines of belief (policies) and the integrity of the opposing characters. Furthermore, by delivering some attacks with a tremendous degree of rhetorical heat, Paul left no room for ambiguity or confusion. He made it clear that he believed his position was right and he could be trusted, and that he believed his opponents' position was wrong and they were unreliable. I would add here that Paul was not just attacking people who disagreed with him; much like Jesus in the gospels, he was attacking those religious figures who seemed to be using their religious authority and position to impose restrictive requirements on the people. It would be impossible to determine if Paul's arguments were correct, but as discursive strategies, the attacks against his accusers adequately serve the purpose of rebuilding the image of his character and policies.

Finally, transcendence was an apt rhetorical strategy. By focusing on the importance of spiritual truth, the unification of all believers, and the eternal struggle between good and evil, Paul directs attention away from the charges against him, in essence denying the importance of the rhetorical attack and defense. Considering Paul's position as a prominent leader in the first-century Christian churches, it would have been inappropriate for him not to have focused a great deal of his discourse on the transcendent issues of faith.

Paul's overall strategy could be distilled to this: "I do not deny that I have taught things some people do not like. I take full responsibility for my words, and I refuse to apologize for them. You should not see my teachings as offensive, because I can be trusted, my opponents are not considering your best interest, and there is a transcendent truth and freedom in what I have to say." Paul's strategies seem to be appropriate choices. Perhaps he could have strengthened his defense with a more straightforward denial of the charges; however, his chosen strategies worked to diminish the offensiveness of his alleged wrongdoings. By limiting himself to reducing offensiveness, he was able to avoid any potential inconsistencies or contradictory tactics. Furthermore, the rhetoric he used provided a meaningful defense of character and policies, while maintaining consistency with his position as a Christian apostle.

Next, it is important to evaluate the effectiveness of Paul's image restoration rhetoric. Since there is no surviving data concerning the extent to which the Galatian believers accepted or rejected the arguments in the letter—although Bruce (1982) claims that after the letter to the Galatians circumcision quickly ceased to be an issue in Gentile mission fields—it will become important to consider how Paul and this document have been treated in religious history.

It appears as though Paul was generally regarded by ancient believers to be an authentic apostle with a legitimate message. Although some of Paul's Jewish Christian opponents continued to circulate damaging documents claiming Paul was a false apostle and a messenger of Satan (see Meeks, 1972, pp. 176–184), the biblical text Acts of the Apostles, and the writings of second- and third-century Christians such as Irenaeus and Tertullian (Meeks, 1972) testify to Paul's general acceptance as a true apostle with an authoritative message. Beyond these evidences and the fact that Paul's letter was canonized as accepted Christian scripture, it is, perhaps, most significant to note that the eventual universalizing of Christianity, spreading to all nations, suggests that a central purpose of Galatians was met.

The specific theology concerning grace that was detailed in Galatians survived as an influential doctrine. Specifically, Martin Luther relied heavily on Galatians in developing his arguments for grace that were brought against the predominant theology of his day (see Bainton, 1950). Moreover, the Pauline doctrine of grace is a ubiquitous belief in contemporary Catholic and Protestant Christendom.

It seems that the *apologia* in Galatians was generally successful. While the legitimacy of Paul's discourse has been debated by giants of theology and philosophy, such as Augustine, Kierkegaard, Nietzsche, Barth, Bultmann, and Buber; various religious figures have taught the theology of Galatians, only to be accused of falsehood and permissiveness by religious opponents (see Bruce, 1982); and the study of Paul's rhetoric has captured the attention of contemporary scholars (Wenham, 1995; Wilson, 1997; Witherington, 1998); the survival of Paul's message in his letter to the Galatians suggests that his rhetoric was an effective form of discourse that sufficiently restored the character and policies of the Apostle Paul.

SUMMARY

In response to perceived accusations that he was a false apostle teaching false doctrine, Paul successfully used the image restoration strategies of bolstering, attacking accusers, and transcendence. With the exception of his omission of a simple denial, these tactics were all effective and appropriate for a religious leader who was seeking to cleanse the image of his character and policies. Furthermore, the clarity of structure and purpose in his defenses removed any ambiguity and promoted a position of epistemic clarity in the dispute. His bolstering worked to establish him as a credible source, and ultimately as a church leader and authority. The attacks against perceived accusers drew clear theological distinctions with soft rebukes for converts, while the harshest assaults were saved for those religious voices who Paul presumed should know better. His transcendence took his discourse to a level beyond simple face-saving. These strategies ultimately proved effective with the public. While it is difficult to establish a causal argument for the success of Paul's discourse, the evidence from ancient, modern, and contemporary religious writings and church practices indicate that Paul's *apologia* was successful as a meaningful piece of religious rhetoric.

What is most interesting about this case is that this was not the image repair rhetoric of a person who simply wanted to be liked more, or who was just concerned with public reputation. However, Paul's defense was also more than a detached, dialectical apologetic for his faith. He used a specific rhetoric with a specific audience to accomplish at least two very important goals. He first sought to establish some clear boundary markers for this new faith by clarifying the difference between the doctrine of grace as a God-centered form of unmerited favor, and the contrasting religious law that was an anthropocentric form of meriting favor through righteous behavior. Another purpose of this *apologia* was to establish Paul as a credible voice in this time of religious revolution. He recognized that his character would be a crucial vehicle for moving Christianity forward among the Gentiles. These issues of grace and individual credibility are arguably components of a Christian rhetoric, particularly of a protestant lineage.

NOTES

1. All references to and direct quotations from the Bible will be taken from the King James Version. Little attention will be given to justifying the Bible as an authentic, trustworthy document. This is not a study aimed at determining what *actually* happened, but primarily about what popular, salient audiences through history and today *believe* happened. Those who find scriptural text suspect will not likely be looking to it as influential with regard to *apologia*. Those who do accept, at least marginally, will not need a protracted defense of it, at least not within the context of a study of this nature.

2. Galatians is generally considered to be the earliest of Paul's letters, and among the most authentic of the Pauline extant (Howard, 1979). It is one of the "undisputed letters" (Witherington, 1998, p. 9), or "capital epistles" (Bruce, 1982), "whose genuineness is beyond reasonable doubt" (Meeks, 1972, p. 1). Even scholars, such as Wilson (1997), who are unsympathetic to Paul's message generally accept Galatians as an authentic Pauline document.

3. Theologians have treated the subject of Pauline rhetoric as an aside. Howard (1979) briefly details the argument that Paul followed a Ciceronian pattern for his letters; Hester (1984) and Witherington (1995, 1998) classify the letters as forensic, deliberative, or epideictic rhetoric; but these works do not follow Brockriede's (1974) admonition to shape rhetorical criticism as an argument.

4. Direct quotations from and references to passages in Galatians are followed by an internal citation listing the chapter and verses.

2

Justin Martyr's Defense of the Persecuted Church

As the apostolic age of Paul was coming to a close, attacks against the Jewish sect—just beginning to be called Christianity—began to intensify. These followers of Jesus faced regular charges of cannibalism, incest, treason, and atheism, as well as other ills believed to be causing the downfall of the Greco-Roman world. The apostolic leaders had for some time responded to conflict within the church communities, but more attacks began to come from outside the church.

Rhetors such as Ignatius, Justin, Tatian, and Tertullian began to publish answers to public accusations from the pagan leaders and intellectuals. These second-century apologists were uniquely interested in cleansing the image of Christianity, rather than primarily proselytizing like their apostolic predecessors. Kennedy writes that "The apologists probably did not expect their arguments to convert the addressees to Christianity—that could happen only through the grace of God—but they could hope to improve the public image of Christianity" (1980, p. 133). And while these advocates worked to preserve their faith, they and their efforts are perhaps immortalized because their rhetoric cost many of them their lives.

Foxe (1989) catalogs the martyrdom of numerous early Christian apologists, among whom Justin has been called the most important (Grant, 1988; Taaffe, 1966). Justin converted from his life as a Platonist philosopher to that of a Christian teacher when he detected fatal errors in Plato's thinking, and when he observed the courage and ease of conscience with which the Christian martyrs were accepting their deaths. Second-century Christians were considered to be a threat to the stability of Roman rule, and were forced to worship pagan gods or face execution. He describes the influence of these martyrs in his *Second Apology*:

> For I myself, too, when I was delighting in the doctrines of Plato, and heard the Christians slandered, and saw them fearless of death, and of all other things which are counted fearful, perceived that it was impossible that they could be living in wickedness and pleasure. (p. 192)

Justin became convinced that the charges that were regularly leveled at the Christians were either completely untrue, or applied only to the heretical sects such as the Gnostics (Grant, 1988), and he worked to defend what he believed was the one true faith.

Justin's *Apologies* have been accepted by scholars (see Roberts & Donaldson, 1907) as perhaps the first systematic defenses of Christianity. As a response to these documents, Justin suffered martyrdom either by hemlock or beheading around A.D. 165 during the reign of Marcus Aurelius. These apologies were clearly influential in shaping the character of Christian belief and practice between the Apostolic age and the Augustinian era. Furthermore, Christian martyrdom has been a recurring theme in history, and has reemerged in contemporary times (Marshall & Gilbert, 1997).[1] As an *apologia* that has essentially been overlooked by rhetorical scholars,[2] Justin Martyr's defense is historically significant, influencing centuries of religious faith and practice.

Where Paul's first-century *apologia* was primarily directed to the community of converts and Jewish-Christian believers, the apologetic literature of the second century was largely aimed at forces outside the church. In efforts to refute charges being made against the new Christian religion, apologists like Tertullian, Tatian, Irenaeus, and Justin made use of classical philosophy and rhetoric to persuade influential Greeks and Romans to cease the persecution and killing of professing Christians. Kennedy (1980) makes note of the fact that, much like Plato before them, many of these advocates used rhetoric to condemn rhetoric as a tool of deception. Furthermore, these second-century apologists made frequent reference to the works of Greek and Roman philosophy in their attempt to demonstrate to the educated, influential members of non-Jewish culture the superiority of the Christian message.

This chapter examines the *First* and *Second Apologies*[3] of Justin as an example of early Christian image repair. As discursive literature similar in some ways to Paul's defense, the *Apologies* are again a blend of apologetics and *apologia* in that numerous arguments contained in the documents advance timeless theological issues as well as character defenses. However, the fact that these discourses are epistles addressed to specific audiences concerning a specific rhetorical context diminishes their character as apologetic dialectic, promoting the case for them as rhetorical *apologia*. Evidence for the rhetorical design of Justin's discourse is demonstrated in the introduction to the *First Apology*:

> To the Emperor Titus Aelius Adrianus Antoninus Pius Augustus Caesar, and to his son Verissimus the Philosopher, and to Lucius the Philosopher, the natural son of Caesar, and the adopted son of Pius, a lover of learning, and to the sacred Senate, with the whole People of the Romans, I, Justin, the son of Priscus and grandson of Bacchius, natives of Flavia Neapolis in Palestine, present this address and petition in behalf of those of all nations who are unjustly hated and wantonly abused, myself being one of them. (p.163)

The introduction to the *Second Apology* also reveals a rhetorical purpose:

> Romans, the things which have recently happened in your city under Urbicus, and the things which are likewise being everywhere unreasonably done by the governors, have compelled me to frame this composition for your sakes, who are men of like passions, and brethren, though ye know it not, and though ye be unwilling to acknowledge it on account of your glorying in what you esteem dignities. (p. 188)

Chapter II of the *First Apology* further situates the discourse, as well as establishes the transcendent tone of Justin's defense.

> For we have come, not to flatter you by this writing, nor please you by our address, but to beg that you pass judgment, after an accurate and searching investigation, not flattered by prejudice or by a desire

of pleasing superstitious men, nor induced by irrational impulse or evil rumours which have long been prevalent, to give a decision which will prove to be against yourselves. For as for us, we reckon that no evil can be done us, unless we be convicted as evildoers or be proved to be wicked men; and you, you can kill, but not hurt us. (p. 163)

This chapter will describe the attacks that prompted these defenses. Justin's image restoration discourse in the *Apologies* will be analyzed. Finally, the effectiveness of his defensive discourse will be evaluated.

THE ATTACKS AGAINST JUSTIN AND THE CHRISTIANS

Since this was a time (ca. A.D. 160) of severe persecution and state-sanctioned murder of Christian believers (Foxe, 1559/1989), it is difficult to point to specific accusations to which Justin was responding. Culling evidence from numerous documents contemporary to Justin's defense, Grant (1988) submits that early Christians were regularly accused by Roman religious, philosophical, and political authorities of sexual promiscuity, offering human sacrifices, cannibalism, and atheism. However, the specific charge for which they received the death penalty was simply answering in the affirmative when asked if they were members of the community of Christian believers. So, in essence there are two classes of accusations being answered. Justin responds to what he perceives to be the significant attacks against the behavior of Christians, and he responds to the class of charges aimed at himself and others for simply professing Christian beliefs.

In Chapter II of the *Second Apology*, Justin provides a narrative example to describe the nature of the attacks and the motivation for his defense. There was a woman, a Christian convert, who sought a divorce from her husband, because of his wicked, corrupting lifestyle. Her husband publicly accused her of being a Christian, and he accused her teacher, Ptolemaeus, of also being a Christian and for corrupting his wife. The prefect, Urbicus, asked Ptolemaeus if he was a Christian, and when Ptolemaeus acknowledged that he was a Christian, Urbicus ordered his death. In defense of Ptolemaeus, a man named Lucius questioned the grounds for such a judgment. Urbicus responded, "'You also seem to be such an one.' And when Lucius answered, 'Most certainly I am,' he again ordered him also to be led away" (p. 189). So, Justin demonstrates the extent to which membership in the Christian community had become accepted as implicitly indicative of social evils deserving capital punishment.

Justin reveals the gravity of the situation, prompting a serious and urgent defense. He was clearly motivated to cleanse both the policies and character image of Christian believers.

A CRITICAL ANALYSIS OF JUSTIN'S APOLOGY

Justin delivers, in the *Apologies*, a significant defense of himself and his fellow Christian believers. Since the text of this *apologia* covers theological issues in great detail and is quite repetitious, attention will be given only to the elements of the discourse that are clearly directed toward the cleansing of Christianity's public image. Justin utilizes the image restoration strategies of denial, bolstering, attacking accusers, and transcendence.

Denial

Justin uses the strategy of denial as a primary instrument for deflecting the specific charges of wrongdoing that were directed toward Christians as a whole. He reveals what he considers to be the most prevalent charges by addressing the accusations of atheism and sexual immorality. However, he also demonstrates the fact that Christians were rarely charged with specific offenses by defending Christian believers against charges of general wrongdoing. This form of denial suggests that the attacks were rarely itemized, but rather assumed as an implicit set of social ills.

Justin's first object of denial is atheism. For the most part, he simply denies that Christians are responsible for atheism when he plainly states in his *First Apology* that they do not "hold these atheistic opinions" (p. 164), and that "we are not atheists" (p. 166). However, his discourse on this issue goes beyond a categorical denial. In a fuller response to the charge of atheism, Justin answers

> Hence are we called atheists. And we confess that we are atheists, so far as gods of this sort are concerned, but not with respect to the most true God, the Father of righteousness and temperance and the other virtues, who is free from all impurity. But both Him, and the Son (who came forth from Him and taught us these things, and the host of the other good angels who follow and are made like to Him), and the prophetic Spirit, we worship and adore, knowing them in reason and truth, and declaring without grudging to every one who wishes to learn, as we have been taught. (p. 164)

Perhaps this argument could be treated as differentiation—distinguishing belief in the Roman gods from belief in the Christian deity as a means of reducing offensiveness—rather than denial. However, since worshipping a Christian god is clearly repugnant to his salient audience, it seems that Justin's argument here functions primarily as a forensic denial of the charge of atheism. He is claiming that Christians are not, in point of fact, atheists because they believe in a god.

Justin next denies the accusation that Christians are sexually immoral. He specifically addresses incest and the prostitution of children in his *First Apology* when he says that Christian believers "shrink from doing any such things" (p. 172). He broadens the denial to sexual impropriety when he claims, "promiscuous intercourse is not one of our mysteries" (p. 172). Justin illustrates this denial by telling a story about a young Christian man who petitioned Felix, the governor in Alexandria, to allow him to be surgically castrated. Felix denied the petition, but the man remained celibate, because he was committed to sexual purity. These claims and the narrative serve to provide a clear denial of sexual offenses.

Justin's final form of denial is directed toward accusations of general wrongdoing. He characterizes such charges as "scattered many false and profane accusations, none of which attach to us" (p. 166). He further denies by referring to the attacks as "scandalous reports against us of infamous and impious actions, of which there is neither witness nor proof" (p. 171). And his denials take on the form of an appeal when he writes, "do not decree death against those who have done no wrong" (p. 186). So, Justin provides repeated simple denials of offensive behavior.

However, his denial takes on a more sophisticated tone when he denies that Christians had done anything wrong when compared to accepted practices of paganism.

> If, therefore, on some points we teach the same things as the poets and philosophers whom you honour, and on other points are fuller and more divine in our teaching, and if we alone afford proof of what we assert, why are we unjustly hated more than all others? For while we say that all things have been produced and arranged into a world by God, we shall seem to utter the doctrine of Plato; and while we say that there will be a burning up of all, we shall seem to utter the doctrine of the Stoics: and while we affirm that the souls of the wicked, being endowed with sensation even after death, are punished, and that those of the good being delivered from punishment spend a blessed existence, we shall seem to say the same things as the poets

and philosophers; and while we maintain that men ought not to worship the works of their hands, we say the very things which have been said by the comic poet Menander, and other similar writers, for they have declared that the workman is greater than the work. (pp. 169–170)

Justin denies offensiveness by demonstrating that Christian beliefs and practices often operate the same as competing beliefs that are tolerated by their opponents. He extends this denial of the accusations against Christians when he argues:

And when we say also that the Word, who is the first-birth of God, was produced without sexual union, and that He, Jesus Christ, our Teacher, was crucified and died, and rose again, and ascended into heaven, we propound nothing different from what you believe regarding those whom you esteem sons of Jupiter. (p. 170)

Again, he claims that Christian belief is not offensive because it shares the same class of belief as the pagan precepts of their opponents. With these arguments Justin provides a denial of the charges of general wrongdoing.

Without ever denying the central charge of membership in the fellowship of Christian believers, Justin repairs the image of Christians by denying the charges of atheism, sexual immorality, and general offensiveness. While this is not his most prominent defense, these denials serve to promote the image of Christians as innocent of the public charges being made against them.

BOLSTERING

Justin attempts to reduce the offensiveness of what it means to be called Christian by bolstering their image. He promotes the credibility of the believers by claiming their philosophical superiority, their humane behavior, and their association with transcendent spiritual truth and power.

First, Justin bolsters the image of Christians by associating the teachings of Jesus with the teachings of Socrates. He begins this argument in the *Second Apology* with his chapter entitled "Christ Compared with Socrates," by claiming,

Our doctrines, then, appear to be greater than all human teaching; because Christ, who appeared for our sakes, became the whole rational being, both body, and reason, and soul. For whatever either law-givers or philosophers uttered well, they elaborated by finding and contemplating some part of the Word. (p. 191)

In essence, he claims that the classical philosophers—Socrates in particular—were partially right, but Jesus, as the divine Word (*logos*), was the complete answer. Furthermore, by adopting this Word as their philosophy, the Christian belief system was intellectually credible.

Second, Justin bolsters Christians by casting them as mutually beneficent. He describes their communitarianism when he writes, "the wealthy among us help the needy; and we always keep together; and for all things wherewith we are supplied" (p. 185). This claim works to refute negative conceptions of Christians by promoting them as caring people, since helping needy people is generally held to be a desirable act.

Third, Justin bolsters the image of Christians by claiming that they possess a lofty goodness by virtue of their beliefs and intimate knowledge of God. In his *First Apology* he writes:

> For as in the beginning He created us when we were not, so do we consider that, in like manner, those who choose what is pleasing to Him are, on account of their choice, deemed worthy of incorruption and of fellowship with Him. (p. 165)

This claim suggests that those who have adhered to God's commands have arrived at a high level of virtue. He goes on, in the *Second Apology*, to claim that this glorified position of Christians actually works to forestall the destruction of the world.

> Wherefore God delays causing the confusion and destruction of the whole world, by which the wicked angels and demons and men shall cease to exist, because of the seed of the Christians, who know that they are the cause of preservation in nature. (p. 190)

So, Christians are more than virtuous; because of them, the world is sustained and God's judgment is forestalled. Justin builds on this depiction of Christians as agents of God's supernatural power when he writes:

> For numberless demoniacs throughout the whole world, and in your city, many of our Christian men exorcising them in the name of Jesus

Christ, who was crucified under Pontius Pilate, have healed and do heal, rendering helpless and driving the possessing devils out of the men, though they could not be cured by all the other exorcists, and those who used incantations and drugs. (p. 190)

So, by describing Christians as incorruptible healers who preserve the world from destruction, Justin significantly bolsters their image.

Justin seeks to mitigate the offensiveness of being called Christian. By creating a vision of Christians and their belief system as philosophically sound, socially charitable, and spiritually powerful, he bolsters the Christian image before their accusers.

Attack of Accusers

Along with denials and bolstering, Justin attacks his accusers in a further attempt to reduce the offensiveness of Christianity. He lodges general attacks against his accusers, describing them as malevolent and offensive. He also accuses them of fundamental inconsistencies and hypocrisy in their attacks on Christians.

Justin presents a laundry list of charges in the *First Apology* when he attacks his accusers for "yielding to unreasoning passion, and to the instigation of evil demons, you punish us without consideration or judgment" (p. 164). Referring to those who punish and kill Christians, he claims they "prove themselves to be wicked, and inhuman, and bigoted. For they kill us with no intention of delivering us, but cut us off that we may be deprived of life and pleasure" (p. 182). He contends that the opponents of Christianity

laugh at us, though they have no proof of what they say, but are carried away irrationally as lambs by a wolf, and become the prey of atheistical doctrines, and of devils. For they who are called devils attempt nothing else than to seduce men from God who made them, and from Christ His first-begotten. (p. 182)

To extend and illustrate these counterattacks further, Justin personalizes his attack in the *Second Apology* by directing his rhetoric at a philosopher by the name of Crescens.

I too, therefore, expect to be plotted against and fixed to the stake, by some of those I have named, or perhaps by Crescens, that lover of bravado and boasting; for the man is not worthy of the name of philosopher who publicly bears witness against us in matters which he does not understand, saying that the Christians are atheists and impious, and doing so to win favour with the deluded mob, and to please them. For if he assails us without having read the teachings of Christ, he is thoroughly depraved, and far worse than the illiterate, who often refrain from discussing or bearing false witness about matters they do not understand. Or, if he has read them and does not understand the majesty that is in them, or, understanding it, acts thus that he may not be suspected of being such [a Christian], he is far more base and thoroughly depraved, being conquered by illiberal and unreasonable opinion and fear. (p. 189)

With these heated comments, Justin is making it tremendously clear that his opponents are culpable for the atrocities perpetrated against Christians; moreover, they are cast as terribly offensive in their thoughts and actions.

Beyond being generally reprehensible, Justin also characterizes his accusers as offensive in their inconsistency of argument and behavior. He attacks the unfairness of their religious persecution when he writes:

Though we say things similar to what the Greeks say, we only are hated on account of the name of Christ, and though we do no wrong, are put to death as sinners; other men in other places worshipping trees and rivers, and mice and cats and crocodiles, and many irrational animals. Nor are the same animals esteemed by all; but in one place one is worshipped, and another in another, so that all are profane in the judgment of one another, on account of their not worshipping the same objects. And this is the sole accusation you bring against us, that we do not reverence the same gods as you do. (p. 171)

This double standard, as Justin describes it, deepens the offensiveness of his opponents' charges. He furthers this argument by claiming that the mythology his accusers hold to is not only unfairly preferred over Christianity, it is corrupt.

But those who hand down the myths which the poets have made, adduce no proof to the youths who learn them; and we proceed to demonstrate that they have been uttered by the influence of the wicked demons, to deceive and lead astray the human race. (p. 181)

By characterizing predominant mythologies as demonic, Justin clearly characterizes his attackers as ignorant, if not malevolent in their practices. Coming to the issue of sexual immorality, particularly the charges that Christians engage in incest and child molestation, Justin turns the argument around on his opponents, claiming that they tolerate such actions among other people and themselves, just not Christians. He writes:

> We see you rear children only for this shameful use; and for this pollution a multitude of females and hermaphrodites, and those who commit unmentionable iniquities, are found in every nation. And you receive the hire of these, and duty and taxes from them, whom you ought to exterminate from your realm. (p. 172)

So the point is made that the beliefs and behaviors of Christians should be viewed as less offensive, because the actions of their accusers betray a basic hypocrisy.

Near the close of both *Apologies*, Justin goes beyond mere attacking to pronounce a judgment on his opponents. In the *First Apology* he writes, "For we forewarn you, that you shall not escape the coming judgment of God, if you continue in your injustice" (p. 186). In the *Second Apology* he claims that "by inflicting on us death or bonds or some other such punishment, as if we were guilty of these things, they condemn themselves, so that there is no need of other judges" (p. 193). Invoking an appeal to a transcendent standard, Justin completes his counterattacks with condemnation.

Justin casts his opponents as generally immoral and hypocritical in their standards of justice. These arguments work to reduce the offensiveness of Christianity by undermining the credibility of its accusers.

Transcendence

While Justin uses the strategies of denial, bolstering, and attack, he clearly relies on transcendence as his primary tactic. His strategy is rather simple; by placing the beliefs and behaviors of his fellow Christians and himself within the larger context of an eternal spiritual reality, Justin hopes to diminish the offensiveness of Christianity. The *Apologies* contain numerous examples of transcendence, some of which are considered here.

In the *First Apology*, he establishes eternity and eternal rewards as a larger context that accounts for Christians refusing to deny their faith:

> It is in our power, when we are examined, to deny that we are Christians; but we would not live by telling a lie. For, impelled by the desire

of the eternal and pure life, we seek the abode that is with God, the Father and Creator of all, and hasten to confess our faith, persuaded and convinced as we are that they who have proved to God by their works that they followed Him, and loved to abide with Him where there is no sin to cause disturbance, can obtain these things. (p. 165)

When considered within this grand context, Justin hopes that the acts of Christians will be viewed as less offensive. Also, he expounds upon the idea of eternity as a kingdom, in which believers do not count their deaths as punishment. He portrays the reality of this life as only a partial reality when he writes,

When you hear that we look for a kingdom, you suppose, without making any inquiry, that we speak of a human kingdom; whereas we speak of that which is with God, as appears also from the confession of their faith made by those who are charged with being Christians, though they know that death is the punishment awarded to him who so confesses. For if we looked for a human kingdom, we should also deny our Christ, that we might not be slain; and we should strive to escape detection, that we might obtain what we expect. But since our thoughts are not fixed on the present, we are not concerned when men cut us off; since also death is a debt which must at all events be paid. (p. 166)

Justin clearly establishes that were it not for this transcendent context, believers would readily deny their faith in order to preserve their lives.

This shift of context brings a radically different frame of reference to the claimed offense of being a Christian. Justin demonstrates that the issue is not about supposed social and political disruptions—it is about disparate views of life and death—when he writes:

Though death is decreed against those who teach or at all confess the name of Christ, we everywhere both embrace and teach it. And if you also read these words in a hostile spirit, ye can do no more, as I said before, than kill us; which indeed does no harm to us, but to you and all who unjustly hate us, and do not repent, brings eternal punishment by fire. (p. 178)

With this argument, Justin suggests that it is not only inoffensive to be called Christian; it is actually offensive to deny it. He goes on to claim that the justification for accepting the label of Christian results in a true freedom when he states:

For we do not fear death, since it is acknowledged we must surely die
... But if they believe that there is nothing after death, but declare
that those who die pass into insensibility, then they become our bene-
factors when they set us free from sufferings and necessities of this
life. (p. 182)

In essence, Justin is denying the offense of Christianity by positioning the attacks as benefits to the faith.

Justin reflects this transcendence in his *Second Apology* as well
when he explains why he and his fellow believers were not denying
their faith:

When we are examined, we make no denial, because we are not conscious of any evil, but count it impious not to speak the truth in all
things, which also we know is pleasing to God, and because we are
also now very desirous to deliver you from an unjust prejudice.
(pp. 189–190)

This commitment to an ultimate truth shows up when he states that
"none of these actions are really ours, and we have the unbegotten
and ineffable God as witness both of our thoughts and deeds" (p.
192); therefore, "we give thanks when we pay this debt [death]" (p.
192). It appears that the transcendence is so profound that Justin's
motives have gone beyond the preservation of reputation in the traditional sense.

By projecting the accusations of the Romans against the broad
backdrop of an eternal, ultimate truth and reality, Justin works to
transcend the issues and reduce the offensiveness of the charges
against Christians. In his transcendent discourse he never mentions
the specific social charges, but focuses entirely on the spiritual transcendence of the Christian faith.

This analysis reveals how Justin used the image restoration strategies of denial, bolstering, attack, and transcendence. Next, it is important to assess the effectiveness of his discourse.

EVALUATION OF JUSTIN'S DISCOURSE

It is first important to note that Justin did not choose to evade
responsibility for the charges, promise to perform corrective action,
or engage in mortification. He chose to deny a certain class of charges
while simultaneously working to reduce the offensiveness of other
alleged accusations.

The strategy of denial was somewhat useful as a response to the accusations of specific acts of social immorality. Justin thoroughly denied the charges of atheism and sexual immorality; moreover, he provided significant denials of general immorality and wrongdoing. These were very serious accusations that called for a response. However, his overall use of denial was weakened by the fact that he did not answer all of the specific charges. Either Justin did not perceive accusations such as human sacrifice and cannibalism as being directed at Christians, or he simply considered them answered in his responses to general wrongdoing. It seems as though such severe attacks should be answered specifically. Furthermore, since there were factions of people—calling themselves Christian, but deviating significantly from central Christian beliefs and teachings—who were practicing some of these offensive acts (Grant, 1988; Taaffe, 1966), Justin could have shifted the blame and deflected the accusations. Overall, his denials were helpful in portraying Christians as innocent, but Justin might have been more specific and could have shifted the blame to more culpable parties.

As was the case with his denials, Justin's bolstering efforts were also mixed in their appropriateness. Perhaps his most meaningful appeal here is his treatment of Christians as philosophically sophisticated, even superior to Greco-Roman philosophers. This would have appealed to his opponents, who were often trained as philosophers. Also, his claims that Christians were socially benevolent would have been attractive to his audience, but much of the benevolence he discussed was contained within the community of believers; therefore, his opponents would not have benefited in any direct manner. His promotion of Christian righteousness was likely his least effective use of bolstering. For bolstering to be effective in reducing the offensiveness of the allegations, it must accentuate qualities in the accused that are valued by the salient audience. To a largely pagan population, Justin's arguments that Christians were good—by virtue of the fact that they were obedient followers of Christ—would have been viewed as somewhat circular and unpersuasive. Therefore, some of the bolstering efforts were fitting, but they did not all work to enhance credibility.

Third, the attacks against the accusers were generally well-conceived. The broad condemnations and the promises of hellfire and damnation were likely of little consequence to his audience; however, Justin's forensic arguments concerning the inconsistencies and hypocrisy in his opponents' positions were probably meaningful to his salient audience. As students of logic and forensic rhetoric, many of his opponents would have had some appreciation for such claims. These attacks at least had the potential of diverting attention away from the supposed offenses of the Christians.

The final tactic of transcendence was a generally effective, but oddly paradoxical, defensive strategy. Responding only to the charge of being Christian, Justin effectively portrayed the issue as much bigger than the Roman social milieu; he diminished the offensiveness of Christianity by describing it as an eternal form of truth. The paradox lies in his argument that the charges against Christianity caused persecution and martyrdom, and that this was actually a blessing. By forming this position, Justin seems to be saying that the accusations should be dismissed; yet without the accusations, Christians are denied the ultimate freedom for which they are thankful. These appeals seem to operate fittingly as transcendence, but not without a certain degree of contradiction.

With the exception of his denial of specific acts, Justin employed the general strategy of reducing offensiveness in response to the charge of being Christian. It seems as though this strategy would have been more complete and effective if he had used differentiation to further separate the social immorality dimension of the charges from the nature of Christianity. Perhaps Justin would have been served best by a two-pronged defense: one approach could have denied the social crimes and shifted the blame to other heretical sects, while differentiating the social behavior accusations from the professed beliefs and practices of "true" Christianity; the second approach would implement bolstering, attack, and transcendence to respond to the charge of being Christian.

Overall, Justin's discourse was fairly well-designed, but incomplete. He needed to create more distinction with new arguments, and he needed to develop more relevance with the strategies he did use.

In spite of some of these weaknesses in rhetorical strategy, Justin's discourse appears to have been somewhat successful historically. He was killed for his beliefs, but his message has been preserved as a model for Christian *apologia* and martyr rhetoric.

Ironically, his death could be viewed as a rhetorical success. Justin was likely beheaded around the year 165 A.D. (Roberts & Donaldson, 1907), thus earning his name, Justin Martyr. His tragic death, coming shortly after the publication of his *Apologies*, suggests that in the immediate context his discourse was a terrific failure. However, it is important to remember that he never counted the avoidance of martyrdom as victory. Much like Blaney and Benoit's (1997) assessment of Jesus' death as a signal of something more than rhetorical failure, Justin's death could be understood as useful in restoring the image of Christianity.

Also, Justin Martyr's discourse has been memorialized as "the most important" of those of the second-century apologists (Grant, 1988, p. 50; Roberts & Donaldson, 1907, p. 160; Taaffe, 1966, p. 12). The influence his rhetoric had on the image of Christianity and the rhetoric of future rhetors positions him well.

Although his rhetorical design was not particularly strong in every respect, and he faced failure in the defense of his personal image, it would be fair to characterize Justin Martyr's discourse as a somewhat successful *apologia*. His defense of Christianity has survived historically as a model of effective apology.

SUMMARY

In response to a variety of accusations made against Christians for social and religious offenses, Justin used the image restoration strategies of denial, bolstering, attacking his accusers, and transcendence. These tactics were well-chosen, but could have been supplemented with blame-shifting and differentiation. Also, the strategies that were used could have been better designed for the salient audience. While Justin's discourse failed to relieve him of guilt in the eyes of his immediate accusers, as a defense of the faith community it was generally successful. As a case of Christian *apologia*, it is held up as a model.

This apology, while arguably not quite as effective as Paul's, utilized a similar range of strategies to diminish the offensiveness of his faith. With the exception of the denials of specific offenses, Justin's program of defense employs the same strategies as the apostolic apology. His use of bolstering demonstrates Justin's recognition that source credibility is of supreme importance is maintaining the integrity and posterity of the faith. By casting himself and his fellow believers as intelligent, charitable, and deeply spiritual, he promotes the image of Christians as a chosen people. His attacks reveal his accusers as moral and intellectual hypocrites. With the transcendent responses, Justin alleges that there is a higher kingdom and a more elevated standard than that of civil authority and respectability. All in all, Justin delivers a Christian *apologia* that takes on a protestantic form by virtue of its defiant tone. Perhaps the style of his image restoration discourse was shaped by the fact that his demise was likely a foregone conclusion. Or, it is possible that for an apology to fit into this lineage I am describing, it must involve an abandoning of prudence and self-preservation in pursuit of deeper conviction.

NOTES

1. The persecution and martyring of Christians is currently practiced in such countries as Sudan, India, China, and Saudi Arabia. It is of value to understand the attacks brought against early Christians and the manner in which they defended themselves so as to understand more fully the oppression in our own times.

2. Sullivan (1998a) mentions Justin's apologies as representative of early *apologia*. Kennedy (1980) briefly mentions Justin Martyr in his treatment of the early Christian apologists; however, he does little more than review the nature of their rhetoric, and he points out that many of the apologists used rhetoric to make their case, while denying the value of rhetoric.

3. While there exists little doubt as to the authorship and authenticity of the *Apologies*, there is some question as to whether they were both part of a single petition, or if they were separate documents (see Grant, 1988). Regardless of the original organization of the messages, this study will treat all of the utterances contained within as a unified program of defense.

3

Here I Stand: Martin Luther's Defense before the Diet of Worms

Luther at Worms is the most pregnant and momentous fact in our history.

—Lord Acton

After the struggles of the early Christians to defend themselves from defamation and extinction, and after the victories of militant Christendom over pagan cultures during the medieval period, perhaps the next most compelling instance of Christian *apologia* is Martin Luther's defense of himself and his doctrine of *Sola Scriptura* at the onset of the Protestant Reformation.

Scott (1942) reports that authority within the Catholic church had been disputed and argued over for 500 years prior to the entrance of the monk, Luther, on the scene. In order to finance the growing appetites of ecclesiastical institutions, the papacy began to sell spiritual indulgences, or remissions of punishment for sins. Luther made public attacks against these practices of the church. While his personal reasons for doing so may never be entirely clear, Luther's subsequent discourse and the discourse of church representatives treated his attacks as a direct response to what he believed to be increasing corruption and secularization within the church.

On October 31, 1517, Luther nailed his ninety-five theses to the door of the Castle Church in Wittenberg, Germany. His arguments concerning papal authority and indulgences in the Catholic church brought criticisms and counterattacks from his fellow monks and scholars. Luther was publicly accused of heresy, and the thrust and parry of these theological disputes grew in size and scope. Eventually, Luther was branded a heretic, excommunicated, and brought before the Holy Roman Emperor, Charles V, and the Imperial Diet of Worms on October 31, 1521, to face charges put forth by Pope Leo X. Jensen (1973) characterizes the trial as the "crucial confrontation of the age" (p. 46). In fact, Luther's defense of himself at that trial and the religious reformation that followed have had a profound effect on the world far beyond that age, making this apology worthy of investigation.[1]

Long before his defense in front of the Diet of Worms in 1521, Martin Luther had adopted a defensive posture in his rhetoric. Through his university lectures, sermons, public debates, and with his historically significant ninety-five theses, Luther had supplied apologetic arguments fueling theological disputes within the Catholic church. As the struggle between the tradition of the church and the voices of reformation became more pointed, and as Luther's image became more of an integral part of the conflict, the rhetoric of attack and defense took on a decidedly personal tone. By the time Luther arrived at Worms, the image of this reforming monk had become of central importance.

It is interesting to note that at the close of the medieval age the tension between religious legalism and Pauline grace arose again as a point of severe conflict within Christendom. Moreover, it is arguable that the impetus for Luther's arguments was found in his preparation of lectures on Paul's epistles to the Romans and Galatians, during his professorship at the University of Wittenberg (Bainton, 1950). As Luther studied these scriptural texts, he became increasingly convinced that spiritual justification was accomplished through faith alone, and that the believer did not need to rely on papal authority. Clearly, this perspective represented a tremendous threat to the Catholic hierarchy, which was teaching that justification was accomplished through the sacraments of the church, often including purchased indulgences. So at the dawn of modernity, the conflict between law and grace is revived, with Luther in the middle, motivated to cleanse his image.

THE ATTACKS AGAINST LUTHER

Most notably, the conflict began in 1517 when Luther publicly denounced numerous practices of the church and papal authority in his ninety-five theses. His most prominent criticism concerned indulgences granted by the church. Indulgences were documents sold by the church enabling the believer to release a loved one from purgatory for a certain number of years, or in some cases, to relieve themselves of guilt altogether. The revenue from indulgences was used to finance church projects, such as the rebuilding of St. Peter's Basilica in Rome (Kittelson, 1992).

Luther was almost immediately pronounced a heretic in a response by Conrad Wimpina, a university professor, and Brother John Tetzel, a Dominican monk who was the administrator over the practice of indulgences in the church. Most of the attacks were simply reiterations of church dogma combined with references to Luther as "'most abominable' 'most impious,' pernicious,' 'insane,' 'blasphemous'" (MacKinnon, 1962, p. 19). Pope Leo X issued a papal bull on November 9, 1518, in which he responded to Luther's attacks on the practice of indulgences, but he avoided directly accusing Luther. Eventually, in June of 1520, Leo X issued the bull, *Exsurge Domine*, in which he condemned the policies of Luther as "heretical, or scandalous, or false, or offensive to pious ears, or seductive of simple minds, or repugnant to Catholic truth, respectively" (Bainton, 1950, p. 113). Although there was some private discussion as to whether the bull should name and attack Luther personally (Olivier, 1978), the bull went on to name Luther as the target: "The books of Martin Luther which contain these errors are to be examined and burned" (Bainton, 1950, p. 114). The bull concluded by giving Luther sixty days to respond or face excommunication. Because the bull was badly flawed in content and structure, Simon (1968) suggests that the bull was a case in point for Luther's arguments against unquestioned papal authority when she writes

> the papal seal was the operative point, excommunication was excommunication, a bull was a bull. It would not be rescinded because it was botched—any more than Luther would have bowed to it had it been a model of the genre. (1968, p. 215)

Luther responded by publicly burning the bull, and six months later Leo X issued his final position in another bull, *Decet Romanum*, formally excommunicating Luther and openly charging him with heresy (Schwiebert, 1950).

Ultimately, Luther was brought before the Diet of Worms to answer these charges before Charles V, the Holy Roman Emperor. Papal advocate Cardinal Hieronymus Aleandro delivered the actual charges in speeches before the Diet. Because the church resented the fact that Luther was even being allowed a hearing, they made their accusation direct so as to limit him to a recantation. Aleandro began the formal accusation:

> Martin Luther, His Imperial Majesty has summoned you here for these two reasons: first to know whether you publicly acknowledge the authorship of the books there before you bearing your name; and then, whether you stand by them or wish to retract anything in them. (Jensen, 1973, p. 46)

The hope was that Luther would have no opportunity to invoke any standards or arguments other than answering the charge of undermining the authority of the church.

So the attacks were made. Luther was clearly held responsible; he repeatedly challenged the authority of the church; his actions against church authority were obviously planned; and as a monk and a professor in the church he surely understood the likely consequences of his contumacy.

In addition, the offensiveness was clear; Luther's statements denying papal authority, his denouncement of indulgences, and numerous other doctrinal positions were determined to be heretical in nature. According to his biographers (see Bainton, 1950; Simon, 1968), Luther's actions were considered by his opponents to be potentially damaging to the church and hypocritical for him as a priest.

Perhaps an analysis of heresy would further describe the nature of the offense. According to Kurtz (1986), the Catholic authorities, religious and secular, viewed heresy not primarily as a violation of God's law, but as a usurping of Catholic authority, which was the representation of God's law on earth. By suggesting such doctrines as justification through faith alone and that individuals could appeal directly to scripture as their authority, Luther had initiated an offensive act against the church. Kurtz submits a theory of "nearness and remoteness" that explains why Luther was targeted. He states that

"Criticism from within a social organization may be more intellectually offensive than external criticism" (p. 11), and that "Mechanisms of control will be activated by elites only when social distance, as well as ideational distance, reaches but does not exceed a critical level" (p. 11). Therefore, since Luther was near as a cleric and scholar within the Catholic church, yet remote as a theological dissident, he was perceived by the church authorities to be a significant threat.

Luther was treated as responsible and offensive by his opponents. In accepting the invitation to appear before the Emperor, Luther demonstrated a motivation to cleanse his image.

A CRITICAL ANALYSIS OF LUTHER'S DEFENSE

Although Luther was very prolific in his published responses to charges brought against him, this analysis will focus on the specific defense he offered during his speeches before the Diet of Worms.[2] Although it may appear that he used differentiation, bolstering, minimization, and attacks against his accusers at times, if taken in context, these strategies serve to promote the two primary strategies of denial and transcendence. Luther's use of these strategies is outlined here.

Denial

Luther's denial works differently than traditional explanations. Ware and Linkugel (1973) refer to denial as a reformative strategy that does not significantly shift the meaning of an offense for the audience. They point out that a denial "consists of the simple disavowal by the speaker of any participation in, relationship to, or positive sentiment toward whatever it is that repels the audience" (p. 276). A simple denial, according to Benoit (1995a), is a matter of claiming, "I did not do it." So, a traditional view of denial holds that the defender accepts the way the auditors view the offense, the defender simply denies involvement. However, it appears that Luther supplied a denial that operates differently. He does not deny the specific actions he is accused of, but he does deny that his actions are heretical.

When questioned as to whether he would claim authorship of all the books attributed to him, Luther appeared to implement the strategy of differentiation. He refused to deny that he wrote the books when he stated, "I must indeed include the books just now named

as among those written by me, and I shall never deny any of them"
(Jensen, 1973, p. 47); in fact, he appeared to use differentiation
further when he stated, "They are all mine, but as for the second
question, they are not all of one sort" (Bainton, 1950, p. 142). With
this response, Luther avoided a yes/no dilemma, and he was allowed
to elaborate. He goes on to clarify:

> There are some in which I have discussed religious faith and morals
> simply and evangelically, so that even my enemies themselves are com-
> pelled to admit that these are useful, harmless, and clearly worthy to
> be read by Christians. (Jensen, 1973, p. 50)

In this answer, Luther seems to be distinguishing between the true
nature of his writings and heresy; except he never specifically designates the difference. Recall that for a defensive tactic to qualify as
differentiation, the rhetor must redefine the supposed offense as something other than what the accusers portray it to be ("This is not what
you think it is."). Therefore, while it appears that Luther attempted
to distinguish between his obviously offensive books and his other
works—avoiding the charge of heresy through differentiation—he
offers a form of denial instead. The essence of his initial defense was
not to reduce the offensiveness of his acts through differentiation, but
to deny the offense by claiming that his books were not heretical.

Luther advances this denial by demonstrating that his books did
not fit the description of heresy. While Ryan (1982) interprets this
move as a differentiation through the stasis of definition, his argument is weakened by the fact that Luther never identified his books
as a unique class of work distinct from heresy; he simply denied that
his works were heretical. Luther separated the books into three
classes. First, there were those that discussed faith and morality.
Luther argued that these books were "useful and harmless" (Jensen,
1973, p. 50), and that to include them in a charge of heresy would
be to condemn "the very truth upon which friends and enemies
equally agree" (Jensen, 1973, p. 50). Second, some books attacked
the papacy, which Luther denied as heretical because the papacy and
the papists, "by their very wicked examples have laid waste the Christian world" (Jensen, 1973, p. 50). Finally, he argued that the remain-
ing books were not heresy because they were directed at private
individuals "who strive to preserve the Roman tyranny and to destroy the godliness taught by me" (Jensen, 1973, p. 51); they were
not aimed at matters of faith. Again, by defining his books as

emancipatory works designed to deflect political and religious oppression, Luther very clearly denies that his actions were heretical, and therefore casts himself as inoffensive.

Perhaps it could be argued that in these denials Luther was actually implementing the strategies of minimization and bolstering. First, he seemed to reduce the offensiveness of the act by claiming that the charges were overstated. Also, it could be argued that he was reducing offensiveness by bolstering his image as an accepted author of theological works. However, it seems that the offense is minimized and his image mildly bolstered as a direct result of the move to deny the charges of heresy, rather than as a deliberate effort to promote his character or to diminish the importance of the offense.

Additionally, it could be argued that Luther was trying to reduce the offensiveness of his books by attacking his accusers, but it seems that he was primarily interested in denying the accusations of heresy by juxtaposing his books from the evil practices of the religious authorities. Granted, his answers cast his accusers as offensive, but his purpose seemed to be a denial of offensiveness through a comparison to the practices of his opponents. It was unlikely that such arguments would transform the reality of his immediate accusers, since they represented the religious establishment he was slandering in his denial. However, it is as if the judicial authorities in the Diet were viewed by Luther as only somewhat salient as an audience. In fact, Ryan (1982) seems to be correct when he argues that Luther's primary audience was not the Diet, but the people of Germany.

Aleandro countered this denial by claiming that Luther was not successful in his attempt to deny offensiveness, because the issue was about Luther's credibility as a heretic. "No doctrine is more effectively deceiving than that which mixes a few false teachings with the many that are true" (Atkinson, 1971, p. 159). Aleandro continued charging that Luther's words were typical tactics for a heretic. He claimed that Luther was arguing "ambiguously... with a logician's evasiveness" (Atkinson, 1971, p. 161). Luther again denied that his rhetoric was subversive within the context of papal authority, but characterized his discourse as a faithful catalyst for healthy dispute in the church: "To see excitement and debate take place because of the study of the Word of God is to me plainly the happiest feature in the whole affair" (Atkinson, 1971, p. 156). Again, he denies that his words are heretical and offensive, demonstrating that his books actually work to provoke debate and serious consideration of scriptural texts.

Luther denied that his actions were truly offensive; he positioned his work as honorable in comparison to the abusive teachings of the church; and he denied that he was engaging in logical trickery and evasiveness, arguing that his discourse provoked meaningful discussion and spiritual growth. He attempted to reform the reality of the situation through a denial of heresy, casting his actions as the efforts of a humble monk to promote healthy theological disputation.

While he never denies performing the specific acts of which he is charged, he denies that those acts were offensive.

Transcendence

Luther attempted to further transform the reality of the situation by employing the strategy of transcendence, which Ware and Linkugel (1973) describe as unique from denial in that it is transformative in nature. By using this strategy, a rhetor hopes to reconstruct, or transform, an audience's reality by situating the act in a new, broader context which redefines the act in reference to a reality different than that previously held by the audience. In general, Luther moved the issue of his books and the charges of heresy into a broader context when he stated, "this is a question of faith and the salvation of souls and because it concerns the divine Word, which we are all bound to reverence, for there is nothing greater in heaven or on earth" (Jensen, 1973, p. 50). It appears that Luther was not attempting to simply cleanse the image of his character. He viewed his defense as a defense for a policy—the cause of Christianity. This move diverted attention away from his own alleged wrongdoings and refocused them on the broader issues. He further cast his conflict with church authorities as a struggle of cosmic proportions when he stated, "If, therefore, I had retracted these writings, I should have done nothing other than to add strength to this tyranny and I should have opened, not only windows, but also doors to such great godlessness" (Jensen, 1973, pp. 50–51). The apparent strategy Luther used here was to transform the meaning and context of the trial by transcending the specific charges and placing them in the larger context of his higher purpose.

Luther's strategy to transcend the context as defined by Aleandro was delineated in one of his speeches, when he clearly shifted the meaning of the trial from an attack against his character and his "heresy" to the larger conceptualizations of politics and the struggle between good and evil:

But, then, I do not set myself up as a saint; neither am I disputing about my life, but about the teaching of Christ. It is not proper for me to retract these books, because by this retraction it would again happen that tyranny and godlessness would, with my patronage, rule and rage among the people of God more violently than ever before. (Jensen, 1973, pp. 51–52)

With this statement, he not only transcended the character and heresy issues, but addressed the political ramifications for the German people. Once again, he seems to be addressing an audience beyond the church authorities seated before him.

Finally, transcendence is found in his last appeal. After Luther had denied the offensiveness of his books and had appealed to the author-ity of scripture, his prosecutor countered by stating that it was a common tactic for heretics to appeal to the Bible. Aleandro reaffirmed the attack and called for a climactic response when he charged:

You have no right to call into question the most holy orthodox faith, instituted by Christ the perfect lawgiver, proclaimed throughout the world by the apostles, sealed by the red blood of the martyrs, con-firmed by the sacred councils, defined by the Church in which all our fathers believed until death and gave to us as an inheritance, and which now we are forbidden by the pope and the emperor to discuss lest there be no end of debate. I ask you, Martin—answer candidly and without horns—do you or do you not repudiate your books and the errors which they contain? (Bainton, 1950, p. 144)

With this question, Luther was faced with a final, unambiguous ulti-matum. In his answer, Luther fully embodied an appeal to broader spiritual and political planes:

Since then your Serene Majesty and your lordships require a simple answer, I will give you one without horns and without teeth, in these words. Unless I am convinced by the testimony of the Scriptures, or by evident reason (for I put my faith neither in Pope nor Councils alone, since it is established that they have erred again and again and contradicted one another), I am bound by the scriptural evidence adduced by me, and my conscience is captive to the Word of God. I cannot, I will not recant anything, for it is neither safe nor right to act against one's conscience. Here I stand! I can no other.[3] God help me. Amen. (Atkinson, 1971, pp. 161–162)

Bringing the conflict to a dramatic crescendo, this statement clearly transcended the context described by his accusers. It is worth noting that Luther gave his answer first in German, to benefit the thousands gathered for the confrontation, then spoke it in Latin for the sake of the Diet. This reinforces the argument that Luther's most salient audience was not the Diet, but the German people. This retort, treated as a singular utterance, transformed the trial from a forum for Luther's humiliation and retraction to a context wherein the conflict between the church and the people was redefined.

The analysis shows how Luther sought to reform the reality of his accusers by denying that his acts were offensive, and how he then worked to transform the reality of the situation by using the image restoration strategy of transcendence. Next, the effectiveness of his discourse is evaluated.

AN EVALUATION OF LUTHER'S DEFENSE

While it is often difficult to sift through the various, and often conflicting interpretations of Luther's words and deeds (see Edwards, 1990), this evaluation will consider two distinct issues. First, the uses of denial and transcendence will be assessed for their strategic rhetorical value. Second, external evidence will be considered as a gauge for the success of Luther's discourse with his various publics.

It is extremely important, initially, to note that Luther, like the other apologists considered thus far, did not attempt to evade responsibility, nor did he promise corrective action, or engage in anything resembling mortification. He supplied a meaningful defense based on the claims that his actions were not offensive, and that his acts were, in fact, something much more than what his accusers thought them to be.

His strategy of denial, while tremendously complex, was an appropriate answer to the dilemma with which he was faced. When he was asked if the books were his, he was being asked to choose the consequences of his heresy or his freedom, which would come at the cost of dishonesty. If he had flatly denied that they were his writings, he would have completely capitulated to the power structure of the church, thus sabotaging his own efforts at reform. Instead, he supplied an intriguing response that seemed to differentiate his writings, in a rhetorical sense, but worked as a denial in a forensic, or legal, sense. By denying the offensiveness of his work, he frustrated the efforts of the prosecution and provided himself the opportunity to speak further in his own defense. This tactic allowed him the chance to rhetorically reshape the reality proposed by his accusers. While this form of denial was not a complete success in eliminating the offensiveness of his acts, it was an effective setup for his next strategy.

The use of transcendence was a very fitting strategy. Perhaps recognizing that he had little to no hope of reversing the positions of his accusers, Luther transcended the issues of heresy, appealing to much loftier ideals. He denied that he was offensive, then he redefined the situation. By appealing to the standards of scriptural authority and individual conscience, Luther tacitly refused the spiritual and political jurisdiction of papal authority and the rule of the Holy Roman emperor. This rhetorical move transformed a civil dispute between church authorities and a renegade priest into a spiritual and political battle of enormous proportions. So Luther's use of transcendence was a useful tool for reducing the offensiveness of his acts.

At the heart of this defensive strategy is the transformation of a salient reality, and a shifting of attention from the audience of authority assembled at Worms to the target audience of the German populace. Perhaps Luther was courageous to the point of inviting martyrdom; but unless it is agreed that Luther was expressing a death wish, his defiance of authority seems to suggest his belief—or at least hope—in a groundswell of support for religious reformation.

The external evidence suggests a mixed result for Luther's discourse. In evaluating Luther's rhetorical defense, it is important to divide his audience into at least two parts. First, his defense was clearly unsuccessful in persuading the Diet of Worms. Almost immediately after the trial was adjourned, Charles V issued a statement signifying his intentions toward Luther: "Henceforth, I shall proceed against him as a notorious heretic" (Jensen, 1973, p. 57). A short time afterward, the Edict of Worms was published by the emperor and the Diet which characterized Luther as a "reviver of old and condemned heresies and inventor of new ones" (Jensen, 1973, p. 75). Luther was officially excommunicated, his books were condemned and ordered burned. Clearly, anything other than mortification that acknowledged the authority of Charles V and Leo X would have met with failure. Ryan (1982) suggests that this had already been decided before the Diet convened. The Pope and the emperor were only interested in a complete retraction; nothing less would suffice. Consequently, when Luther refused to recant when faced with the charges, the issue was over in their eyes. Therefore, due to the deep conflict over authority and the nature of truth, Luther's denial of heresy and his transcendent discourse had no effect on the governing authorities.

Luther's efforts were received differently by the German public. While the Diet of Worms was an important audience, it is arguable that the most salient audience to Luther was the German people. The immediate public response to the trial was so clearly in support of Luther that the Pope's advocate, Aleandro, was afraid to stay in Worms after the publishing of the Edict (Jensen, 1973). Luther's transcendent "Here I stand" speech has been characterized as "brief and bold" (Jensen, 1973, p. 52), "a linchpin of Christianity, of the human spirit and of history" (Olivier, 1978, p. 167), "its reverberations still resound throughout Christendom" (Schwiebert, 1950, p.167). However, it succeeds as a tool of image restoration as well. Through the use of transformative rhetoric that so clearly contrasted the reform position with that of the existing church, Luther successfully reduced the offensiveness of his behavior. In spite of the Edict of Worms, the Reformation spread rapidly throughout northern Europe over the next few decades. Some joined the movement for political or economic reasons; however, Jensen (1973) suggests that many were converted to Luther's way of thinking theologically as a result of his rhetoric before the Diet. Edwards (1990) argues that Luther's rhetoric, most notably his speeches before the Diet of Worms, contributed to the inciting of the Peasants' War of 1525. Clearly, Luther's discourse was meaningful to the German people.

In addition to historical accounts which could be skewed by perspective and presupposition, a way of calculating Luther's success can be found in the amount of Luther's work that was published. Edwards (1983) maintains that while it is nearly impossible to gauge the precise influence of historical rhetoric such as Luther's, he suggests that a means of evaluation can be found in the public demand for published work. During the sixteenth century, printing was possible but difficult and expensive. Therefore, it can safely be assumed that works that were published were in high demand. Although this is at best an indirect measure, and it could be influenced by a number of nonrhetorical factors, Edwards (1983) claims the fact that Luther's polemic and theological works were published hundreds of times serves as a relatively reliable indicator of his success.

The evidence suggests that, while Luther failed in the immediate context of the Diet of Worms, his image restoration discourse was successful with his salient audience, which Luther apparently perceived immediately. In a letter following the Edict of Worms, Luther reflected on the consequences of his rhetoric:

> I will continue to polish the truth and make it shine, and the more my unmerciful lords scorn me, the less I will fear them. Neither of us is over the mountain yet, but I have the advantage that I am traveling unburdened. God grant that truth keep the victory. (Hendrix, 1981, pp. 136–37).

By avoiding the strategies that would fundamentally have confirmed his opponents' view of reality, Luther denied offensiveness and used the transforming strategy of transcendence to reshape reality and provide an impetus for one of the most significant religious and political movements of all time.

SUMMARY

Martin Luther employed a significant rhetorical defense of his image before the Diet of Worms. He used a variegated version of denial and the strategy of transcendence in an attempt to change the reality of the situation and reject the charges of offensiveness that were brought against him. These tactics appear to be well-chosen, given that he seemed to be targeting the general public, primarily, rather than his specific accusers. While he was not successful in repairing his image before his immediate audience, the people of northern Europe validated Luther's overall success. Furthermore, the proliferation and endurance of Luther's message during the sixteenth century and beyond promote the belief that his image restoration strategies were successful.

Luther's apology was fascinating, particularly his peculiar use of denial as a tactic. It was as though he slyly bundled differentiation, minimization, bolstering, and attacks against his accusers, and delivered them as a denial. In a strictly rhetorical sense, Luther used all of those strategies; but, the final function for the accusing audience was as a denial. He was not simply trying to diminish the impact of his actions; he sought to go beyond that and flatly deny that he was a heretic. Even Aleandro remarked about the perplexing "trickery" of such a move that achieved rhetorical goals for his broader audience but met the legal needs of his immediate predicament. And, like those who went before him, Luther transcended the issue, placing his actions in the context of a truth that was higher than church authority. This *apologia* was clearly representative of protestantic rhetoric, as it is considered one of the signature pieces of rhetoric from the Protestant Reformation.

We reach a point at which I should comment on the discourse of the these first three historical cases. It is remarkable how the situations faced and the strategies chosen by these three rhetors are so similar. In each instance, the accused is subject to attack, perceived or explicit, that is directed at some religious belief or practice that opponents have determined to be illegitimate. Therefore, all three offer a defense of their character, only as it is a manifestation of their faith (policies). Furthermore, each rhetor is facing some sort of censure, even potential execution, for their offenses. And perhaps most important, each of the three is performing at a crucial juncture, a defining moment, in the history of the Christian faith. Paul is shaping the doctrinal concepts of early Christian identity within the community of believers; Justin is seeking to preserve a culture of belief that is facing potential destruction; and Luther is defining a radically new perspective in the midst of a centuries-old tradition.

In these similar rhetorical situations, our three historical apologists are amazingly consistent in their choices of image restoration strategies. The Apostle Paul bolsters, attacks his accusers, and transcends; Justin Martyr uses some denial along with bolstering, attacking, and transcendence; and Martin Luther employs a form of denial that incorporates other strategies, as well as transcendence. With some minor variations, they use a uniform program of defense.

These chosen strategies begin to give shape to a religious rhetoric, particularly an historical, protestantic Christian rhetoric. I submit that the texture of such historical religious discourse involves the following characteristics. First, rhetors create sharp distinctions between their beliefs and the practices of opponents. Rather than standing on the shoulders of giants, these figures are seeking to separate themselves from traditional views they see as destructive. In all of their strategies, they stress how they are different.

They also promote individual credibility and authority. The character and competence of the speakers, and the groups they are associated with, need to be unassailable if their message is to be imbued with integrity. Moreover, the amount of emphasis that is placed on personal faith and revelation invites a move away from hierarchical church authority.

Next, these historical examples all transcend the status quo, asking their audience to stop looking at things from a certain point of view, and inviting them to a new perspective. They all seem to be acting out Paul's encouragement, "And be not conformed to this world: but be ye transformed by the renewing of your mind, that you may prove what is that good, and acceptable, and perfect, will of God" (Romans 12:2). This is significant as a challenge to the status quo; but it also exalts the role of the individual in knowing and performing God's will, separate from the authority of others.

Finally, this form of rhetoric seems to be delivered with the doctrine of grace as a subtext, and with a broader audience in mind than that of the immediate auditors. These rhetors seem to believe that the laws imposed by corrupt civil and religious bodies can be overruled in an appeal to a universal favor that is granted by God to all who believe. In addition, the sanctions—perceived or real—threatened by the accusers are undercut when the target audience reaches far beyond the actual accusers. It is as though these rhetors are saying, "The real standard is beyond you and your rules, and the real audience is beyond you and your ability to harm me."

NOTES

1. Few communication scholars have examined the rhetoric of Luther. Scott (1942) reviews the high-profile debates Luther engaged in before his final break with papal authority. This study provides a helpful historical-rhetorical context for Luther's *apologia*, but it contributes little to our understanding of how Luther argued, or how rhetoric functions in a religious milieu. Besides passing footnote reference in Kruse (1977) and Ware and Linkugel (1973), the only communication study that specifically treats Luther's *apologia* is Ryan (1982). Ryan argues that Luther's defense must be interpreted within the context of papal attack; moreover, Ryan argues that Luther's discourse must be viewed as a defense of policy rather than character. However, Ryan does not consider Luther's apology as a component of Christian rhetoric; the rhetoric is treated in much the same way as political self-defense discourse. Luther's *apologia* deserves further study because his discourse has not been analyzed within the framework of a general theory of image restoration, and the uniquely Christian dimensions of his apology have not been considered.

2. There are few English translations of his complete works. Therefore, the texts that were consulted comprise a variety of translations and compilations of Luther's discourse. Although this might create some inconsistency in translation and interpretation, the artifacts used were consistently treated in all of the resources.

3. Most of the translations claim that the statement "Here I stand! I can no other" was part of a manuscript prepared before Luther journeyed to Worms. It appears possible that it was added into the account of the trial by some translators, although it is uncertain whether Luther actually said these words during the trial.

Part II

The Contemporary Apologists

4

Sin, Sex, and Jimmy Swaggart's Sermonic Apology

Jimmy Swaggart, the cousin of rock and roller Jerry Lee Lewis and country singer Mickey Gilley, was once the champion of the "electronic church" (Abelman & Hoover, 1990, p. 1). During the 1980s, Swaggart became one of the world's most widely watched Christian televangelists (Frankl, 1987; Hadden & Swann, 1981), claiming over two million weekly viewers in more than 140 countries ("Swaggart Agonistes," 1988). Before facing a public sex scandal in 1988, he was one of the most influential voices in religious media.

While he may have been committed to the spreading of the faith, Swaggart was also interested in attacking those who he felt were contravening the goals of his gospel. He frequently served as self-appointed inquisitor accusing communists, homosexuals, pornographers, Catholics, Jews, hypocritical Christians, and various other groups and individuals of sinful behavior; and in 1987 he was instrumental in exposing the sexual misconduct of rival televangelists Jim Bakker and Marvin Gorman, which led to both men being defrocked by the Assemblies of God. Only months later, the tables were turned as Swaggart, himself an Assemblies of God minister, found himself before the general presbyters after Gorman turned over photographs that showed Swaggart at a hotel with a known prostitute. His tearful confession from the pulpit of the Family Worship Center in Baton Rouge, Louisiana, was a significant media event, which was followed by regular stories on the evening news for several days.

While appearing on the surface to be little more than fodder for tabloid journalists, Jimmy Swaggart's apologies merit scholarly attention for several reasons. First, the impact of Swaggart's rhetoric as a religious leader was significant in size and scope; most of his rhetoric of image repair was played out before an international audience. Second, Swaggart's defense is regularly compared to that of other public figures, like former President Clinton (Carlson, 1998). Third, Swaggart's *apologia* has not been sufficiently studied by communication scholars,[1] and provides a tremendously public example of a Christian figure facing a need to repair his image.

Unlike his historical counterparts, Jimmy Swaggart's apology was prompted by accusations of behavior unrelated to his beliefs and practices as a religious leader. He was not defending a theological precept or the policies of Christianity; nor was he attempting to preserve the image of a dissenting faction. Instead, he found himself faced with charges of personal immorality, specifically sexual misconduct. However, his program of defense was conceived and communicated as religious rhetoric. Swaggart was not just a man accused of misdeeds who just happened to be a religious figure; he used the language of religion to exonerate himself.

In this example of contemporary *apologia*, mass media played a significant role in the creation of the event and the communication of the subsequent image restoration discourse. Swaggart initially faced accusations as a result of his playing the role of self-appointed moral inquisitor during the scandals of fellow televangelists, and was repaid when one of them (Gorman) returned the favor by launching an investigation of Swaggart that resulted in serious allegations and Swaggart's ultimate downfall. Schultze (1991) suggests that the relatively new and supremely powerful medium of television produced a great deal of tension as religious figures competed for resources. In this case, religious media served as the site of the original sins and the promise of salvation.

This chapter describes the accusations brought against Jimmy Swaggart and his subsequent attempts to restore his badly damaged reputation. Swaggart's defensive rhetoric is analyzed, with specific attention given to the nationally broadcast apology on February 21,

1988 (Simonds, 1990). Finally, the effectiveness of the televangelist's discourse is assessed.

THE ACCUSATIONS AGAINST JIMMY SWAGGART

After contending that the charges levied by Swaggart were the source of his fall from prominence and the loss of his credentials as an Assemblies of God minister, Gorman hired a private investigator to spy on Swaggart. Hackett (1988) reports that the investigator took photos of Swaggart visiting a prostitute at a New Orleans motel, then let the air out of one of Swaggart's tires and called his employer. Gorman came to the motel disguised in a baseball cap and sunglasses, and identified Swaggart while he was changing the tire. "Gorman kept the incident quiet for four months, hoping—he claims—Swaggart would come clean on his own" (Hackett, 1988). Gorman finally delivered the pictures to church officials, and the attack against Swaggart was official.

On February 18, 1988, Swaggart appeared before the General Council of the Assemblies of God in Springfield, Missouri to answer charges of sexual immorality. The primary substance of the attack was found in the photographs supplied to the presbyters. However, the accusation was corroborated a few days later when a prostitute named Debra Murphree stepped forward claiming to have had regular motel meetings with Swaggart for more than a year. She acknowledged that she was the woman in the photos and that Swaggart was a sexual pervert that she wouldn't want her children to be around (Ostling, 1988, March 7). While much of the accusation against Swaggart relied upon implications rather than outright claims, the attack clearly portrayed him as guilty of illegal and morally reprehensible behavior. Church leaders were critical of Swaggart and suggested that his credentials might be in danger.

In this situation, there was little question that Swaggart, the accusing parties, and the general audience viewed Swaggart as responsible. The statements from the prostitute also establish the perception that the act was offensive because it was calculated and had occurred many times before.

The accusations against Swaggart were particularly poignant in this regard because of the perceived hypocrisy. While prostitution and pornography might be offensive enough to some segments of society, when a minister who claims to be a moral agent in society flagrantly violates the moral standards he upholds, the resultant contradiction can significantly damage his credibility. In addition, Swaggart only months earlier had successfully charged Gorman of sexual immorality (Hackett, 1988) and in the aftermath of Jim Bakker's sex scandal had referred to Bakker as "a cancer on the Body of Christ" (Hackett, 1988, p. 30). Apparently, the inconsistency of standards contributed to the vilification of Swaggart in this situation. Clearly, the attack against Swaggart established him as blameworthy for an offensive act. These two conditions being met, Jimmy Swaggart faced a serious threat and was therefore motivated to attempt to cleanse his image.

CRITICAL ANALYSIS OF SWAGGART'S IMAGE RESTORATION STRATEGIES

Jimmy Swaggart reportedly confessed to the charges before the presbyters by saying, "Here I am. I'm sorry . . . I'm at your mercy. I love you all" (Hackett, 1988, p. 30); however, his formal public program of defense began three days later from the pulpit of the Family Worship Center in Baton Rouge, Louisiana. The televised confession on February 21, 1988, was widely covered by the media (Hackett, 1988; Ostling, 1988, March 7; "Preachers Who," 1988; Rosellini, 1988; "Swaggart Is," 1988).[2] While Swaggart's televised confession gained a great deal of national attention, further image repair efforts included an audiotape he mailed out to supporters, as well as articles Swaggart wrote in his monthly magazine, *The Evangelist*. He initially used mortification and bolstering. In addition, he employed the strategies of defeasibility, minimization, attacking accusers, and differentiation as his program of image restoration progressed. Since they follow a loose chronology, the strategies will be analyzed in that order.

Mortification

The televised confession is the only occasion in which Swaggart publicly admitted wrongdoing without qualification. He accepted the accusations to be an accurate assessment of the situation, and he confessed his offenses in public by repeated statements of concession. He supplied a general confession and an apology to the specific audiences he felt he had harmed. However, as his program of defense unfolded, Swaggart began to incriminate himself less.

He began his televised confession by stating bluntly and without reservation, "I do not call it a mistake, a mendacity, I call it sin"

(Simonds, 1990, p. 108). He went on to establish culpability and take complete responsibility for the offense by stating, "I have no one but myself to blame. I do not lay the fault or the blame or the charge at anyone else's feet" (p. 108). With these statements, he accepted the blame and the offensiveness of the situation, making no effort to explain the situation, excuse himself, or diminish the seriousness of his behavior. It is further important to note that, at this point, he makes no attempt to revise the events as they had been reported.

In addition to his admission of guilt, Swaggart continued his repentance by addressing those he believed he had harmed. In his appeals to his family, the Assemblies of God denomination, the members of his ministry organization, fellow evangelists, followers, and God, he acknowledged his offense against them, the harm it caused them, and actively sought forgiveness. He repeatedly made statements like, "I have sinned against you," and "I beg your forgiveness" (pp. 110–112). Again, by engaging in a confession, he made no effort to reshape the nature of the offense or his involvement.

However, as his program of defense developed, Swaggart's confession was modified. In his taped address, mailed out to supporters in August 1988, Swaggart accepted responsibility for the event when he said, "I take full responsibility for what actually did happen" (Simonds, 1988, p. 119). Nevertheless, in that same month's issue of *The Evangelist*, Swaggart wrote, "I do not in any way try to evade the responsibility. But, at the same time, that sin was forgiven and washed by the blood of Jesus Christ and personally (and eternally) forsaken" (1988e, p. 6). This apology, while technically behaving as mortification, attempts to soften the impact of the offense through a self-proclaimed exoneration.

While his mortification was forthright and appeared to be sincere, it is interesting to note two things. First, Swaggart never identified the particular nature of the sin; consequently he repented for behavior that was never actually defined and that he assumed his audience was aware of. Second, he qualified his confession by inserting a claim of absolution into the apology. By admitting his wrongdoing, Swaggart worked to convince his audiences of his sincerity in the hope that he would be pardoned.

Bolstering

Swaggart sought to reduce the offensiveness of his acts by bolstering his image. He did this by first appealing to the style of religious image and discourse his audiences would appreciate. He then associated himself with prominent biblical figures in an attempt to elevate the perception of him as a man of God.

First, he bolstered himself by appealing to "the Pentecostal ethos" (Blumhofer, 1988, p. 333) by establishing himself as a strong, truthful, and honest source speaking from a spontaneous emotional perspective rather than a rationally constructed text. He began his televised confession by saying, "Everything that I will attempt to say to you this morning will be from my heart. I will not speak from a prepared script" (Simonds, 1990, p. 108). Projecting a defiance not unlike that of Martin Luther, he said, "I have never sidestepped or skirted unpleasantries. I have tried to be like a man and to preach this gospel exactly as I have seen it without fear or reservation or compromise" (p. 108). By identifying himself with and reinforcing the basic concepts upon which his particular brand of fundamentalism was premised, and by reminding his audience of his tenacious commitment to their particular brand of truth, he attempted to reduce the offensiveness of his acts by bolstering himself and reshaping his image. By performing his apology sans script, he projected the image of the Pentecostal preacher who does not rely on prepared statements that are prepared through a process of consultation and reflection, but who relies solely on the inspiration and guidance of the spirit.

The most notable method Swaggart used to bolster his image was identifying himself with biblical figures. In his televised speech and in various articles, he created a parallel between himself and the Old Testament figure, King David. In his televised speech he said, "God said to David three thousand years ago, 'You have done this thing in secret, but I will do what I do openly and before all of Israel'" (Simonds, 1988, p. 110). In the biblical narrative, David, the king of Israel, was forgiven by God after committing adultery with Bathsheba, and went on to enjoy a long and prosperous reign. Swaggart related his experience to the Davidian reference by stating, "My sin was done in secret and God has said to me, 'I will do what I do before the whole world'" (p. 110). He ended his speech by reading Psalm 51, which is David's confession and appeal to God. In addition to his references in the speech, Swaggart wrote articles (1988a, 1988e) that further developed a link between his experience and David's struggles as King of Israel. Clearly, Swaggart hoped the audience would associate his situation with David's fall and subsequent reemergence to greatness, and forgive him as God had forgiven the Israelite king.

In addition to David, Swaggart later compared his struggles and imperfections with those of the disciples Peter, James, and John. "So we're talking about real men, with all the warts and wrinkles peculiar to frail humanity—not men of flawless spiritual development" (1988c, p. 7). Perhaps he felt that if his audience could associate his failures and redemption with these esteemed figures, he could rehabilitate his image as a great disciple of God.

His attempt to reduce the offensiveness of his acts through bolstering is apparent when he repeatedly compared his untoward behavior with the fallibility of great spiritual leaders of the past. Thus, Swaggart's program to repair his image through bolstering was found in his association with a familiar religious ethos, and by associating himself with familiar and well-respected biblical figures.

Defeasibility

As his defensive discourse progressed, Swaggart attempted to evade responsibility for his admitted wrongdoings. He introduced the strategy of defeasibility when he suggested that his indiscretion was the result of nerve problems and an addiction.

First, he claimed that his failures resulted from physical and mental fatigue when he wrote, "I do not blame anyone for the past mistakes except Jimmy Swaggart, but I do know when one works from total exhaustion week after week and month after month, there will be a breakdown of some kind" (1988b, p. 12). He proceeded to refer to some vague sort of breakdown that he never described in detail. "I did not break down physically or spiritually. It came from another direction" (1988b, p. 12). Clouding his claims in ambiguity, he put part of the blame on his breakdown.

Second, Ostling (1988a) reported that Swaggart suffered from a self-professed addiction to pornography, which made him less resistant to sexual temptation. The confession of this addiction works to place his actions somewhat beyond his volitional power.

The claims of breakdowns and addiction may have been intended to evade some responsibility, or perhaps these claims of defeasibility were simply attempts to establish an ambiguity about the situation that would enable future image repair efforts. Nevertheless, Swaggart attempted to evade full responsibility for the behavior by attributing the act to forces beyond his control.

Attacking Accusers

Months after the initial confession, Swaggart began to use attacks to reduce the offensiveness of his behavior. While he never directly attacked the central players in his downfall (Gorman, Murphree, or the Assemblies of God officials), he launched general attacks against a broad sweep of accusers. He never named particular individuals, but he claimed that rival preachers and secular media were attempting to destroy his television ministry. He wrote in March 1988, "Some wanted us off for political reasons, some for personal reasons, and some for spiritual reasons. They were fabricating all types of lies to weaken our financial base" (p. 5). He continued his attacks against the media in June and December of 1988. Moreover, he accused fellow Christians of hypocrisy when he suggested that they were failing to welcome him back into the fold as a forgiven brother (1990, p. 3). In an attempt to diminish the offensiveness of his original untoward behavior, Swaggart diverted attention from his offense to the transgressions of his opponents. Interestingly, he sought to redefine the situation as the ongoing conflict after the original act, rather than the original act itself.

Differentiation

Through his use of differentiation, Swaggart attempted to distinguish between the public perception and the actual offense. Aided by his ambiguous mortification that failed to designate the specifics of his offense, he hoped to reduce the offensiveness by changing the perceived nature of the act.

Swaggart separated the act that was frequently reported to the public from the actual offense when he wrote, "What I *actually* did, which was not what the news media said, I take full responsibility for" (1988, December, p. 10). The differentiation was amplified later when he wrote that "what actually happened had little resemblance to what was portrayed over television, was reported in the press, and was fantasized by some preachers" (1989, p. 7). Clearly, Swaggart was attempting to reduce the offensiveness of the act by separating it from the larger context of sexual immorality.

However, much like his reference to an ambiguous "breakdown," Swaggart never provided details of exactly how his actions were dissimilar from what was reported. Suggesting that the difference was an issue of intent, he wrote, "I did not intentionally disobey, but there was one area that I did not quite understand" (1988d, p. 8). He may have been referring to his public claim, reported by Ostling (1988a) that, while pornographic acts were performed, he never actually had intercourse with the prostitute. However, his failure to explain the differentiation leaves the issue in ambiguity.

Unlike the previously mentioned defenses, the attempt at differentiation was an attempt to completely transform the nature of the offense in order to reduce the offensiveness of the act in the eyes of the salient audience.

It appears that Swaggart's *apologia* moved progressively, yet decidedly, from contrite discourse in which he repented and asked forgiveness, to more ambiguous rhetoric designed to partially evade responsibility and reduce offensiveness. In the first stages of his defense, he adhered closely to his audience's perception of him and the act by engaging primarily in mortification; however, as his defense progressed, he seemed to reshape the meaning and reality of the situation by using bolstering, defeasibility, attack, and differentiation. Next, it is important to assess the effectiveness of these strategies.

EVALUATION OF SWAGGART'S RHETORIC

It appears that Swaggart's defense was largely unsuccessful. Although he managed to partially salvage his ministry in the face of certain ruin, the effects of his image repair rhetoric did little to reverse the decline of his image. In order to support this evaluation, the appropriateness of the image restoration strategies Swaggart chose will be examined. Next, speculation is advanced about how Swaggart could have developed his program of defense more effectively. Finally, external reactions to and from Swaggart are discussed as a means of corroborating this evaluation of the effectiveness of his defense.

In the face of overwhelming evidence, Swaggart never attempted to directly deny the charges against him. Although he was vague at times, he initially chose to accept full responsibility for the offenses with which he was charged, later shifting to strategies aimed at evading responsibility and reducing offensiveness. He also did not engage in transcendence, as did the historical apologists. Perhaps his awareness of his guilt prevented him from such a strategy.

The five strategies of mortification, defeasibility, bolstering, attacking accusers, and differentiation separately represent potentially useful image repair efforts. If the actor is guilty, it can be very effective to conform to the audience's perspective and confess the offense. In light of the confession, it can also be beneficial to reshape the audience's perception of the responsibility of the accused by claiming circumstances beyond normal control. Similarly, the rhetor can effectively diminish the impact of the attack if the audience's perception of the offense is changed by bolstering the image of the accused and by attacking the accusers. Also, the offensiveness of the event can be reduced if the rhetor can separate the reality of the event as distinct from the original accusation. Therefore, since Swaggart never attempted to deny the accusations, these strategies provided an opportunity to acknowledge guilt while saving face.

Swaggart's defense was developed in two phases, the first of which was his televised confession[3] in which he primarily confessed and bolstered. Schultze (1991) characterizes the media confession as "a masterful stroke of video, organized visually and aurally around the biblical theme of forgiveness" (p. 39). In the speech, Swaggart defined his audience as his family, his followers, his denomination, his colleagues, and God. Recognizing that his salient audience was deeply religious and responsive to messages presented with spiritual fervor, Swaggart did not submit a statement or press release. He delivered a sermon.

Blumhofer (1988), explaining the effectiveness of Swaggart's apology in the context of a Pentecostal audience, writes, "The appeal for forgiveness and unconditional support is the part of their heritage that responds to remorse, tears and dramatic testimonies" (p. 334). When Swaggart placed such an emphasis on deliverance through confession and forgiveness, he was tapping into the very doctrines that comprise the core of Pentecostalism. What is interesting is that he did not attempt to reduce the offensiveness of the act by transforming his audience's concept of the act. Instead, the prevailing ethos of his followers allowed him to use the untoward nature of the offense *to his advantage*.

Inasmuch as his sermonic apology was effectively developed within the context of a religious ethos, the second phase of his defense was weaker. By locating a portion of the responsibility in forces beyond his control, by attacking his accusers, and by differentiating his acts, Swaggart departed from this sermonic program. It is difficult to accept the contrition and his association with noble religious figures as consistent with the later strategies. Perhaps this was the difference between authentic confession and staged confession. Kruse (1977) suggests that religious individuals who truly seek God's forgiveness have no need to justify their behavior to others. If his confession was not entirely genuine, Swaggart may have felt the need to supplement it with other efforts. This move seems to betray the authentic Pentecostal ethos he invoked previously.

Swaggart should have remained consistent with his sermonic apology. Blumhofer (1988) suggests that within the rhetoric of Pentecostalism is the idea that sin is and should be met with immediate consequences. Therefore, in order for Swaggart to remain consistent with this perspective, he needed to maintain the strategy of mortification, acknowledging his moral failures, and waiting for redemption. Additionally, he could have adopted the strategy of corrective action, or penance, as a means of "paying for his sins." While ambiguity can sometimes allow room for image revitalization, his strategies seemed to weaken with the lack of specificity. He never specifically admitted what he had done. He was vague about the forces that were beyond his control (was it the devil? sexual addiction? blackmail?). And the accusers that he attacked were never named. His refusal to be specific about his immorality and his later strategies designed to absolve him of responsibility estranged Swaggart from the religious sentiments that he had initially invoked to save himself. Therefore, his early strategy of contrition or his later strategies might have been successful if they had avoided ambiguity and if he had not tried all of them. This cocktail of conflicting strategies only served to prompt confusion at best and distrust among many.

While he appears to have been successful in choosing his early rhetorical strategies, his program of defense was unsuccessful at eliminating all of the consequences of the offensive event. Judging Swaggart's sermonic apology to be genuine, on the day after the confession, officials for the Louisiana district of the Assemblies of God ordered a soft punishment of three months' suspension from preaching and a two-year rehabilitation program (King, 1988). However, the general council, after receiving more than 10,000 calls demanding harsher penalties, rejected the ruling of the district officials and mandated tougher sanctions (Woodward, 1988). The presbyters finally ruled that Swaggart could not preach behind a pulpit or in front of a camera for one year (Ostling, 1988b). He defied the ruling ("Jimmy Swaggart," 1988; "Swaggart defies," 1988), continued his protracted program of defense, and was officially defrocked in April

("Swaggart Goes," 1988). Clearly, the loss of his ministerial credentials suggests that his defense was certainly not successful with an
important contingent of auditors.

Swaggart went on to preach and conduct his ministry, but without denominational affiliation. The ministry reported a $1.5 million
decline in contributions in April 1988 (Abelman, 1990). Over the
next two years, his television ministry fell from the top position, and
his program was dropped by 200 television stations around the world
("No Apologies," 1991). The pages of his magazine, *The Evangelist*,
were reduced by over seventy-five percent, and fund-raising appeals
appeared to become more desperate as they grew to include pleas for
supporters to include the ministry in their wills.[4] The contrast with
his success before his fall from prominence is stark.

While Swaggart managed to maintain a severely downsized ministry in the aftermath of these events, his marginal survival may be a
result of events unrelated to his defensive discourse. In general, it is
clear that Jimmy Swaggart's image repair efforts were largely unsuccessful.

SUMMARY

Jimmy Swaggart employed a significant rhetorical defense of his
image. While his initial use of mortification and bolstering may have
eventually proven effective, his later program of defense seemed to
contribute to his failure. By engaging in defeasibility, attacking
accusers, and differentiation, Swaggart seemed to evoke a form of
apologetic ambiguity and strategic confusion that damaged his
reputation-building efforts. Withdrawing from his early sermonic approach that promised to expunge him of guilt before his religious
audience appears upon critical reflection to have been a fatal error
in rhetorical judgment.

Swaggart's discourse was ineffective with most of his audience. The
denominational authorities revoked his credentials, his television
outlets were severely reduced, the financial health of his ministry
operation was significantly impaired, and the overall size of his audience fell off considerably. As difficult as it is to develop causal relationships between instances of *apologia* and their effects, this
prolonged program of defense seems to have ended in failure.

As a case of contemporary apology, Swaggart's defense demonstrates the impact mass media can have on the evolution of a strategy.

If he had only been able to deliver one speech before a large audience, or publish one significant essay in response to the charges, Swaggart might have come out of this scenario with quite a different result. However, the capacity of print and electronic media to produce new messages, almost daily, prompts the apologist to consider modifications when the original line grows tired.

All of this seems to suggest that a meaningful protestantic Christian rhetoric should remain consistent with the religious ethos; and it should preserve some sense of rhetorical cohesion in order to succeed. Swaggart initially moved in the right direction by recognizing the need for confession, and drawing attention to the redeeming power of grace. He also recognized the importance of source credibility for those who teach about faith. In this case, however, Swaggart seems to have taken the protestantic dimension of Christian rhetoric too far. By declaring himself absolved of his sin, claiming that this was an issue that was strictly between him and God, and by ignoring the authority of church leaders, Swaggart shifted the focus so much onto himself that his discourse severed him from the community of faith in which he relied for his shelter. The ethos of forgiveness and redemption was his hope for image restoration; the paradox was that by shifting the focus almost entirely onto his character, away from the content of the faith (policies), his efforts began to fail.

NOTES

1. Pullum (1990) has analyzed how Swaggart's media message generated mass appeal, but no published study has analyzed his *apologia*.

2. Transcripts of Swaggart's televised confession and his audiotape comments can be found in Simonds (1990, pp. 108–121).

3. Although it is not within the scope of this study to analyze the speech from a media perspective, Schultze (1991) provides a detailed analysis of camera usage, off-camera audience reactions, etc.

4. From a review of *The Evangelist* from 1988 to 1991.

5

Jesus Crisis: Controversy in the Search for the Historical Jesus

For the last 150 years, there have been cyclical, punctuated phases of scholarly interest in the historical Jesus—as distinct from the Jesus of traditional Christian faith (see Crossan, 1991; Witherington, 1997). The first search, spanning the last half of the nineteenth century, is characterized by Albert Schweitzer's seminal work, *The Quest for the Historical Jesus* (1968), originally published in 1906. The second inquiry, chronicled in the works of Bultmann (1934) and Robinson (1959), lost momentum in the 1970s. Fueled by new data, refined historical-critical methodologies, and a renewed level of interest, the third quest began in the early 1980s. This third quest, which is ongoing, became an issue of public interest in the mid-1980s when a group of iconoclastic biblical scholars formed the Jesus Seminar.

Robert Funk, a well-respected New Testament scholar, founded the Jesus Seminar in 1985 under the auspices of his Westar Institute. Co-chairman John Dominic Crossan, professor emeritus at DePaul University, joined him from the beginning. Funk and Crossan along with approximately seventy other fellows of the Jesus Seminar began convening twice a year to discuss gospel texts and vote on what they believe Jesus actually said.

That in itself is not unique from other scholarly gatherings, but the Jesus Seminar is different in that its meetings and publications have become well-orchestrated media events that often begin with strong attacks against traditional Christian orthodoxy. As an example, Funk (1996), in the prologue to his book, *Honest to Jesus*, refers to traditional believers as "compliant, mindless adherents of the received tradition" (p. 12), and he casts their positions of faith as the "hypocrisy of pastors and parents who either did not know the truth or refused to divulge it" (p. 12). So the distinction of this third quest for the historical Jesus is that it targets popular audiences through a media-savvy message that is occasionally perceived as an attack on fundamentalism and televangelists as much as it is seen as a case of traditional scholarly polemics.

The conflict over the historical Jesus continues to generate major media attention with hundreds of newspaper articles,[1] public radio broadcasts (Crossan, 1998), network news spots ("Clash between," 1996), and public television coverage (Mellowes, 1998). Since Jesus of Nazareth is one of the most influential figures in human history, and since public perception of him and his followers has a tremendous cultural impact, consideration of this modern controversy demands our attention. The manner in which the Jesus of traditional faith is defended in response to the antagonism of historical research deserves attention as an object of study because it represents faith-based discourse being used to answer charges grounded in naturalistic, scientific discourse.

While the Jesus Seminar has provoked the ire of evangelical Christian scholars and laypeople since its inception, the conflict reached a fever pitch with the publication of Luke Timothy Johnson's vitriolic response, *The Real Jesus* (1996), and with the cover stories in the Easter 1996 issues of *Christianity Today* (Edwards, J. R., 1996), *Newsweek* (Woodward, 1996), *Time* (Van Biema & Ostling, 1996), and *U.S. News & World Report* (Sheler, Tharp, & Seider, 1996), which brought focus to the efforts of the Jesus Seminar and the reactions of its detractors.

The agenda of the Jesus Seminar stands in stark contrast to the aims of Christian conservatives and traditionalists.[2] The Jesus Seminar is dedicated to publicizing a view of Jesus based on historical and scientific analysis rather than faith systems and creedal statements. The fellows of the Seminar contrast their efforts with the views of conservative Christian scholars, arguing that traditionalists use the unreliable texts of the Synoptic Gospels (Matthew, Mark, and Luke) to create Jesus in their own image. The Seminar, therefore, operates under a general rule of evidence that states, "Beware of finding a Jesus entirely congenial to you" (Funk et al., 1993, p. 5).

In order to generate some sort of intersubjective consensus about their findings, the Seminar gathers semi-annually to vote on the authentic words and deeds of Jesus. Their often-criticized voting method involves the casting of colored beads. A red bead means, "Jesus undoubtedly said this or something very like it." A pink bead means, "Jesus probably said something like this." Gray means, "Jesus did not say this, but the ideas contained in it are close to his own." And black beads mean, "Jesus did not say this; it represents the perspective or content of a later or different tradition" (Funk et al., 1993, p. 36). With methods such as these, Funk, Crossan, and their associates seek to bring their version of Christological skepticism out of the confines of academia and into the popular spotlight. The consequence is a growing rhetorical conflict between those who promote the Christ of faith and those who are focused on the Jesus of history.

Before continuing with an analysis of this rhetorical dispute, it is important to make two observations. First, at the core of the conflict between the Jesus Seminar and Christian traditionalists are contrasting epistemologies. While a thorough discussion of the types of competing epistemologies can be found elsewhere (see Evans, 1996; Wolterstorff & Plantinga, 1983; Wood, 1998), for the sake of introducing this case it is sufficient to describe the epistemology of traditionalists as embracing the possibility, even likelihood, of supernatural acts and the authority of the Christian scriptures and the gospels in matters pertaining to faith and history. The epistemology of the Jesus Seminar involves a shift in the burden of proof, wherein supernatural activity and the accuracy of the scriptures are assumed to be in error unless proven otherwise through methods of critical historiography. Johnson (1996) describes this polarity when he writes,

One perspective views Christianity as based in God's self-disclosure or revelation, and therefore structured and enlivened by the self-disclosure. In this view, Christianity is regarded as a way of life rooted in and organized around a genuine experience of ultimate reality mediated by the crucified and raised Messiah, Jesus. The other perspective sees Christianity as another among the world's religions, that is, fundamentally as a cultural reality rooted in the human construction of symbolic worlds. (p. 57)

Seminar members acknowledge this presumption when they describe their "methodological skepticism" as "a working principle of the Seminar: when in sufficient doubt, leave it out" (Funk et al., 1993, p. 37). "From this point of view, the 'faith perspective' of the texts themselves must be countered by a 'hermeneutics of suspicion'" (Johnson, 1996, p. 58). This presuppositional disagreement sets the stage for dramatic and pointed epistemological conflicts.

The second important item of note is that the substance of the conflicts between the Jesus Seminar and traditionalists is primarily communicated as apologetics: dialectical arguments that are timeless in their application. The disputes over ontological and epistemological premises, while important in informing and shaping the arguments, are not the primary focus of this study. While elements of the dialectical arguments will creep into the analysis, this project is designed to illuminate the rhetorical aspects of the Jesus Seminar's specific attacks on traditional Christian belief, and the particular *apologia* put forth by contemporary defenders of traditional Christianity.

This chapter examines the accusations made by the Jesus Seminar[3] and its fellows against the character and policies of conservative Christian believers. The defensive discourse of various conservative Catholic and Protestant rhetors will be analyzed as image restoration discourse. Finally, the effectiveness of the traditionalist *apologia* will be evaluated.

THE JESUS SEMINAR ATTACKS

This chapter is unique in that it is difficult to determine exactly when the attacks began or who is responsible for the first volley. It is admittedly arbitrary to define the Jesus Seminar as the attackers and traditionalists as the defenders, as the following analysis will perhaps indicate. However, it seems that the statements and publications of the Seminar were the first specific attacks to capture public attention. Most traditionalist attacks followed the Seminar's lead.

In his keynote speech at the first official meeting of the Jesus Seminar, Funk (1985) makes the initial accusations against traditional Christianity when he says, "The religious establishment has not allowed the intelligence of high scholarship to pass through pastors and priests to a hungry laity." He then goes on to claim that "the radio and TV counterparts of educated clergy have traded in platitudes and pieties and preyed on the ignorance of the uninformed. A rude and rancorous awakening lies ahead." Organizing the Seminar as a vehicle of attack, and recognizing that their efforts will be taken as offensive to many, Funk continues, "What we are about takes courage. . . . We are probing what is most sacred to millions, and hence we will constantly border on blasphemy. We must be prepared to forebear the hostility we shall provoke." These opening comments assign blame to a certain brand of Christian leaders for deceiving their followers. These words also reveal Funk's awareness of how the Seminar's efforts will be viewed as an attack on traditional Christian belief. It is interesting to observe that he expects counterattacks as the rhetorical response from his targets.

Funk continues generating a significant amount of rhetorical heat aimed at traditional believers when he describes conservative church officials as more concerned with membership numbers and revenue than with historical accuracy (see Johnson, 1996). Funk charges traditionalists with historical corruption by claiming that "the church adapted Jesus to fit its needs" (1989, p. B8). Perhaps his most revealing personal attack comes when he considers the impact of the epistemological conflict between historical analysis and faith: "The only Jesus most people want is the mythic one. They don't want the real Jesus. They want the one they can worship. The cultic Jesus" (1994, p. E6). As the organizer and leader of the Jesus Seminar, Funk's comments operate as attacks on the beliefs and practices of traditional Christianity.

After Funk's initial provocations, the Seminar worked collectively to determine the historicity of Jesus' words, which resulted in the publication of *The Five Gospels: The Search for the Authentic Words of Jesus* (Funk, Hoover, & the Jesus Seminar, 1993). With this book the Seminar launched the first significant attacks as a group.[4] Among the numerous arguments and charges it brings against traditional belief, it first maintains that those who believe in the inerrancy of the gospels often claim infallibility as a method for establishing doctrinal authority. "It is for this reason [the establishment of authority] that some churches were moved to claim infallibility for their interpretation. And it is for the same reason that televangelists and other strident voices have made equally extravagant claims" (p. 6). The impact of this claim, according to the Seminar fellows, is that those who think they are in possession of absolute truth have no room for faith.

The next important position staked out in *The Five Gospels* is the distinction between the Jesus of history and the Christ of faith. The Seminar finds that the church "appears to smother the historical Jesus by superimposing this heavenly figure on him in the creed" (p. 7). The fellows lay the specific blame on "the dictatorial tactics of the Southern Baptist Convention and other fundamentalisms" (p. 8). By insisting on the primacy of Jesus' "mythical role" (p. 7), the traditionalists are viewed as obscuring the truth.

Among the many substantive objections to the Christ of faith and to what the fellows consider the largely fictionalized narratives of the gospels, the members of the Seminar lob a final accusation in the introduction to *The Five Gospels* when they claim that "Latter-day inquisitors among Southern Baptist and Lutheran groups have gone witch-hunting for scholars who did not pass their litmus tests" (p. 35). They characterize their opponents as unqualified when they anticipate counterattacks from "those who lack academic credentials" (p. 35). So the Seminar establishes a substantive difference from traditional believers, going on to name some and challenge their ethics and abilities.

While there are numerous other members of the Jesus Seminar whose published works indict traditionalists (see Borg, 1994; Crossan, 1991 for instance), they do little more than repeat the charges from Funk and the Seminar. What is perhaps more relevant here is the perceptions traditionalists have of the attacks.

Scholars representing traditional Christian faith generally agree that the Jesus Seminar accuses traditional belief for being offensive in one way or another. Johnson (1996), a chief opponent of Funk and the Seminar, perceives their efforts as provocative in nature when he characterizes the project as an "effort by scholars to bypass the ordinary contexts of their activity in order to effect cultural change by direct competition with conservative Christians" (p. xi). Moreover, Johnson supports the idea that the initial attacks originated with the Seminar when he claims that they intentionally provoked traditionalists in order to create media events: "All that was needed for the culture wars to begin was to fire the first salvos and await return fire from the churches" (p. 11). Some among traditionalists view the attacks as being against the character of Jesus himself as well as against traditional believers (Wilkins & Moreland, 1995). Evans (1996) describes the activities of the Jesus Seminar as particularly damaging to traditional belief in its divorcing of the historicity of Jesus from his divinity. In a broad summary of the Seminar's critical scholarship, Johnson (1996) gathers the major claims of the Jesus Seminar into a grouping of constant traits that he perceives as attacks on traditional Christian belief and scholarship. While most of these traits are dialectically apologetic in nature, in one of the traits Johnson declares the common attack: "They state in one way or another that traditional Christianity is a distortion of the 'Jesus movement'" (p. 55). He goes on to argue that the attacks are particularly damaging because they do not come from religious outsiders; for the most part, the attackers are in some way identified with Christianity.

It is important to recall Kurtz (1986), who posited that heresies, or damaging claims against faith, were worsened by their "nearness and remoteness." The fact that Jesus Seminar members are usually faculty in religion departments, teachers of New Testament studies, or clergy, contributes to their nearness: they are intimate in knowledge and experience with the Christian faith. However, their rejection of the traditional gospel narrative as historically and spiritually authoritative positions them as remote: standing outside the fold of "true" believers. This unique position makes the Seminar's accusations significant as claims against traditional belief.

Therefore, the attack is made. The words of the Jesus Seminar are generally accepted by their opponents and themselves to be a form of accusation against the policies and character of traditional Christianity. The heart of the attack is essentially found in the separation of the historical Jesus and the Christ of faith—a crisis of dueling epistemologies. Conservative believers are considered to be responsible for championing faith at the expense of historical truth. Furthermore, traditionalists are characterized as narrow-minded and deceptive in their understanding and practices. Next, the attacks are strengthened by their nearness and remoteness. Lastly, it is interesting to note that most of the content of *kategoria* is located in introductions, opening comments, and early chapters that serve as preludes to other substantive arguments; they are rarely the central purpose of the discourse. Overall, the Jesus Seminar's attacks are perceived as casting traditionalists as responsible for systematically corrupting the minds of their followers with incorrect and potentially damaging falsehoods. Opponents of the Jesus Seminar are clearly motivated to respond.

A CRITICAL ANALYSIS OF THE TRADITIONALISTS' DEFENSES

Few specific individuals or groups are named in the Jesus Seminar's attacks, and even fewer of those named provide specific responses to the charges. Therefore, the apologists considered here are primarily scholars working in much the same setting as members of the Seminar, but who happen to embrace a more traditional Christian faith perspective. They are not surrogate defenders—like Hillary Rodham Clinton was for her husband, the accused president—because the attacks are leveled at them as traditional believers. However, their stakes in the *apologia* are not as significant or direct as those considered in previous chapters. That is not to say these apologists are not motivated to provide image restoration.

There is clearly a motive for image repair. In a personal sense and within a cosmic perspective, these traditionalist rhetors clearly feel compelled to respond. Wilkins and Moreland (1995) portray the importance of defending a faith position.

> We are not overstating it when we say that these are life and death issues. The most important elements about any belief we may have about any topic are that the belief is really true and that we have good reasons for thinking it is true. (p. 6)

They continue by demonstrating the effect traditional Christian belief has on the perception of image.

> If Jesus is who he claimed to be and who his followers declare him to be, then we are not dealing simply with academic questions. We are instead dealing with the most important questions of the modern person's daily life and eternal destiny. If he is not who the Bible declares him to be, then we are simply fooling ourselves if we hold to traditional beliefs. (p. 11)[5]

Since humans are fundamentally motivated to be right and not to be thought fools, the stage is set for the restoring of image.

The nature of this conflict as a dialectical struggle between two polemical extremes promotes a generous use of attacks against accusers. However, these apologists also utilize a form of denial, bolstering, differentiation, and transcendence.

Denial

Traditionalists' simple denials are anything but simple. As they defend their faith system from the contemporary challenges of the Seminar, their specific rhetorical responses blend with timeless apologetics that transcend historical setting. Most of the specific denials are dialectical rebuttals to issues of history, interpretation, and method; therefore, they do not qualify as *apologia* in the strictest sense. For instance, Evans (1996) contends that the incarnational narrative, or the traditional gospel story, does not necessarily violate the standards of critical historiography. Meier (1991) agrees that Jesus was a marginal Jew and a scandal to his contemporaries, but he denies that this precludes Jesus from being the resurrected Messiah. In response to Seminar claims that longer gospel teachings and parables could not be attributed to Jesus because they had to be transmitted orally, Bock (1995) argues that the Jewish culture of memory and orality makes it possible for such messages to be kept intact over time.[6] Traditional scholars and spokespeople develop an apologetic, providing voluminous denials to the substance of Seminar claims.

Taken alone, these types of arguments are difficult to receive as *apologia*; however, treated as a collection of popular and scholarly responses to the Seminar's rhetorically situated attacks against traditional Christianity, these rebuttals could be understood as image-restoring denials. Taken together as a whole, they seem to answer the charges of historical inaccuracy and deceptive and manipulative teaching.

The fact that these studies are offered by credentialed scholars seems to answer the accusations that traditionalists are uneducated and incapable of historical or textual analysis. In fact, Witherington (1997) advances the credibility of traditional scholars when he writes that

> Evangelicals who use the historical-critical method tend to read all of the significant literature on the subject, and their writings reflect this familiarity with the relevant scholarly literature written by people of all sorts of faith and of none at all. (p. 257)

In another context this claim might be construed as bolstering; however, in this case it is used to answer the direct attacks of the Jesus Seminar that their traditional opponents were uneducated and academically incapable.

While direct denials of specific charges are rarely ever provided, the opponents of the Jesus Seminar repair the image of traditional Christianity by denying the charges of deception and ineptitude. This is far from their most substantial *apologia*, but this program of denial supports the restoration of traditional Christianity's public image.

Attacking Accusers

Opponents of the Jesus Seminar deny many of the attacks against them, but their most significant image restoration strategy is found in the numerous and heated attacks against their accusers, which take many forms. Traditionalists submit attacks against the motives of particular members of the Seminar. They also attack the Seminar for what they see to be questionable academic credibility, flawed methodologies, and the corrupting of religious truths.

Johnson (1996), widely considered to be the primary popular opponent of the Jesus Seminar, attacks specific Seminar members Marcus Borg, John Dominic Crossan, and Burton Mack; however, he reserves his hottest rhetoric for Robert Funk, whom he calls "the *magister ludi*, the coordinator of the game" (p. 13). In much the same way that Funk and the Seminar members characterize traditional Christian leaders as deceptive and dishonest in their motives, Johnson casts Funk similarly when he says, "It is important to note from the start that Funk does not conceive of the Seminar's work as making a contribution to scholarship but as carrying out a cultural mission" (p. 6). Witherington (1997) extends this personal invective when he attacks Funk's motives in writing his book, *Honest to Jesus* (1996). "Funk says his book is about setting Jesus free from his dogmatic and ecclesiastical cages, but it sounds more like Funk's effort to free himself from those 'cages'" (p. 276). Both of these examples demonstrate how traditionalists wish to portray the Jesus Seminar as missionary-minded, rather than detached and objective.

Next, Johnson (1996) continues his frontal assault on the Seminar with a volley of caustic statements. He characterizes the *Five Gospels* as "second-rate scholarship" (p. xi). Disturbed by the Seminar's crafting of media-friendly images and events, he accuses them of engaging in "a ten-year exercise in academic self-promotion" (p. 1), which he later refers to as "a self-indulgent charade" (Johnson, p. 26). Turning to somewhat more substantive comments, he refers to the Seminar's research as "repetitions, non sequiturs, and narcissistic self-referentiality" (p. 33). He also argues that the Seminar does not engage in historical research when he claims that its members contribute nothing new and they make grossly subjective assessments. "It is a paper chase, pure and simple. It is, indeed, like a house of cards" (p. 99). With comments like these, Johnson is clearly interested in painting as dark a picture as possible to describe the Jesus Seminar.

Several critics undermine the academic pedigree of the Seminar membership by attacking their academic qualifications and by suggesting that the membership is not representative of the community of biblical scholars. Witherington (1997) points out that the organization is not sponsored by the Society of Biblical Literature or the Society for the Study of the New Testament. After a detailed review of the membership, he goes on to claim that the Fellows of Seminar are "hardly a representative sampling of critical scholars" (Witherington, 1997, p. 44). Citing the lack of scholarly publications and lack of academic diversity, Johnson maintains that "the roster of the fellows by no means represents the cream of the New Testament scholarship in this country" (1996, p. 3). Blomberg (1994) concurs when he argues that the Seminar is "not even representative of mainstream contemporary New Testament scholarship," and that at best the membership "reflects the 'radical fringe' of critical scholarship" (online). These comments work to damage the reputation of the accusers by questioning the credibility of the Seminar's scholarship.

The next object of attack is the Seminar's unusual method of arriving at scholarly decisions by holding votes that are cast with colored beads. Johnson calls this voting mechanism "a deliberate attention-creating device" (1996, p. 5). Witherington (1997) goes further in suggesting that the voting process, which is promoted as democratic, actually denies fairness and equal representation of viewpoints. He argues that,

> While the voting may make the process *appear* democratic, the preselection of the fellows, the exclusion of the majority of scholars, the disregard for the vox populi and, perhaps most tellingly, the disregard for the opinions of scholars of previous generations, shows that we are dealing ultimately with an elitist and not a democratic approach. (p. 45)

In fact, Witherington demonstrates that because of the four grades of bead colors (red, pink, gray, and black) and the voting method, numerous gospel passages are determined to be inauthentic, with only a small percentage of the Seminar membership voting black ("Jesus did not say this."). With these attacks against the voting and the beads, traditionalists seek to undermine one of the most publicly mediated trademarks of the Seminar's activities.

In response to the attack that traditional Christianity ignores the Jesus of history to favor the Christ of faith, traditionalists counter-attack the Seminar for unfairly dichotomizing history and faith. Johnson (1996) contends that "The Jesus Seminar exploits this popular distinction when it speaks of historical deliberations delivering 'the real Jesus' in contrast to the 'Christ of faith,' who is by implication somehow less than 'real'" (p. 81). After Seminar member Crossan (1995) claims that reason and history are superior to revelation and faith, and that reason should always be our final judge, Witherington (1997) replies hotly, "What this means in practice is that faith must be constantly redefined according to the latest historical reconstruction of the facts" (p. 272). Wilkins and Moreland (1995) lay the responsibility for this history-faith split at the door of what they describe as the Seminar's philosophical naturalism. After attacking this position at length on substantive grounds, they extend their comments to attack the Seminar's *a priori* rejection of the traditionalists' epistemology when they claim that "such a commitment [to naturalism] is Procrustean in that it often forces the evidence of history to fit an unjustified antisupernatural bias" (p. 10). According to Johnson, this prejudging form of inquiry is responsible for research that is "biased against the authenticity of the Gospel traditions" (1996, p. 5), causing him to claim that "the game was rigged" (p. 14). So the traditional counterattack to the history-faith issue is that the Seminar is equally guilty, if not more so, of denying the Christ of faith in favor of a falsely created Jesus of history.

The final attack, which contains more severe moral and spiritual impacts, is brought by Wilkins and Moreland (1995) when they claim that the Seminar's activities are tremendously harmful to the spiritual well-being of their listeners:

> They are not only intellectually insufficient, but they leave people spiritually bankrupt and hopeless. If we adopt the portrait of Jesus that is offered in some of their works, we have simply a wise teacher, a religious sage, a pious spinner of tales and proverbs, a revolutionary figure, a Jewish peasant and Cynic preacher, or a spirit-person. This is the kind of Jesus who cannot offer eternal salvation or the power to live life as we know we should. (1995, p. 231)

Such a comment is clearly designed to persuade audiences sympathetic to Christian faith that the harms of traditional faith are of no consequence in comparison to the corrupting work of the Jesus Seminar.

In summary, the advocates of traditional Christian faith and scholarship attack their accusers, the Jesus Seminar, in an attempt to reduce the offensiveness of the Seminar's original arguments. The traditionalists attack the Seminar's leaders, motives, credentials, and methods in an attempt to diminish their credibility and thereby enhance the credibility and public image of traditional Christian belief, practice, and scholarship.

Differentiation

Since part of the Seminar's charges against traditionalists rests in the claim that the historical Jesus is ignored or misconstrued, Johnson (1996) works to reduce the supposed offenses of traditional Christianity by differentiating between religion that portends to assemble and worship a historical figure and religion that worships a living, present being. His central claim is that the charges of the Jesus Seminar have little impact, because the Seminar thinks traditionalists are doing history poorly, when they are doing something entirely different. In an attempt to clarify this point, Johnson writes,

> Christians direct their faith not to the historical figure of Jesus but to the living Lord Jesus. Yes, they assert continuity between that Jesus and this. But their faith is confirmed, not by the establishment of facts about the past, but by the reality of Christ's power in the present. Christian faith is not directed to a human construction about the past; that would be a form of idolatry. Authentic Christian faith is a response to the living God, whom Christians declare is powerfully at work among them through the resurrected Jesus. (1996, p. 143)

The essence of this argument—which is not shared by all traditional apologists (see Witherington, 1997; Wright, 1996)—is that, while the Jesus of history is alive and well and congruent with traditional theology, the faith of traditional Christianity is not dependent on the verifiability of the historical Jesus. It is as though he is arguing "We are not *referencing* history, we are *making* history." This distinction is of critical importance if the nature of the offense is the poor treatment of history. By differentiating the practice of faith from the practice of history, Johnson seeks to reduce the offensiveness of the Seminar's accusations.

Transcendence

Nearly all of the traditional apologists incorporate transcendence near the end of their published discourses. As a move to restore the image of Christianity and deflect the charges of the Jesus Seminar, traditionalists appeal to the larger, more expansive issues of belief and eternity. Evans (1996) suggests that beyond all the struggles between faith and history, there are issues of greater importance.

> The most effective apologetic arguments may be those that aim to show that the story of Jesus contains the solution to life's deepest problems, and to show that eternal life with the God Jesus reveals is what human beings at bottom really want. In so far as humans are sinful, as Christianity claims, then it will also be true that the story contains what humans do *not* want: the truth that they are not their own gods, but are responsible to their Creator. In that case, the very offensiveness of Christianity may be seen as one indicator of its truth. (pp. 354–355)

This argument transcends the charges of the Jesus Seminar by placing the conflict within a larger context of truth and human need.

Wilkins and Moreland (1995) follow this pattern by supplying an entire conclusionary chapter devoted almost entirely to diverting attention from the dispute to proclaiming the primacy of Jesus as the hope of humankind. Johnson refines this idea in the context of the history-faith dichotomy. Is what is claimed to be a pursuit of the historical Jesus not in truth a kind of flight from the image of Jesus and of discipleship inexorably ingrained in these texts?

> For our present age, in which the "wisdom of the world" is expressed in individualism, narcissism, preoccupation with private rights, and competition, the "wisdom of the cross" is the most profoundly countercultural message of all. Instead of an effort to rectify the distorting effect of the Gospel narratives, the effort to reconstruct Jesus according to some other pattern appears increasingly as an attempt to flee the scandal of the gospel. (1996a, p. 166)[7]

By redefining the issue to be about the evangelistic message of the gospel instead of the defense of the faith, Johnson transcends the issues.

Johnson proceeds to transcend even further. After supplying a thorough reaction to the Seminar's historical, epistemological, and methodological positions, Johnson (1996) ironically suggests that, not only should traditionalists transcend the issues raised by the Jesus Seminar, they should not engage in typical apologetics at all.

> The more the church has sought to ground itself in something other than the transforming work of the Spirit, the more it has sought to buttress its claims by philosophy or history, the more it has sought to defend itself against its cultured despisers by means of sophisticated apology, the more also it has missed the point of its existence, which is not to take a place within worldly wisdom but to bear witness to the reality of a God who transforms suffering and death with the power of new life. (p. 168)

Thus, the traditionalist apologists transcend the charges leveled by the Seminar by looking past the details of the academic and ecclesiastical conflict and declaring that their efforts are aimed at the spiritual transformation of humanity. Through these efforts at transcendence, the apologists seek to reduce the offensiveness of traditional faith.

EVALUATION OF THE DEFENSE

It is difficult to offer a comprehensive assessment of this *apologia*, because the apologists make little effort to identify whom their target audiences are. Therefore, the primary purpose of this evaluation section will be to consider the cogency and logical consistency of the arguments. The external persuasiveness of the image restoration discourse will be considered as well, but the effect on the audience is impossible to determine with much reliability, since so many potential audiences are involved.

The discourse of the traditionalist Christian apologists contains elements of denial, attacking accusers, differentiation, and transcendence. The opponents of the Jesus Seminar never act to evade responsibility for their faith or actions, nor do they communicate any remorse for their supposed offenses. Their arguments serve to deny the accusations and reduce the offensiveness of the public claims.

The denials were moderately successful as replies to the charges. The traditionalist apologists thoroughly and systematically address the substantive historical arguments proffered by the Seminar. To the extent that traditionalists considered these issues in an even-handed, scholarly fashion, and provided *prima facie* responses to the central arguments, they denied the attacks of the Seminar. By addressing the issues and publishing their positions they denied the claims that they were deliberately obscuring the issues and withholding information from the public. Also, the involvement of seemingly well-credentialed scholars in the traditionalist endeavors seems to answer the direct and perceived charges of academic weakness and shoddy scholarship. However, the denials could have been stronger. Since the Seminar's attacks often originated in character assaults, the traditionalist respondents should have isolated these charges and provided unambiguous denials of them, separate from the substantive historical and philosophical arguments. Second, blame could have been shifted to the popular Christian voices that are not particularly representative of traditionalist scholarship and practice. Johnson (1996) comes near this when he critiques televangelists, fundamentalists, and radically conservative Christian professors for their extreme views, but he stops short of scapegoating them. Overall, the apologists' denials work to partially restore traditional Christianity as innocent of the Seminar's charges; however, they could have organized and clarified their responses more effectively, and they could have assigned blame to more responsible parties.

The traditionalists' attacks against their accusers were equally mixed in their appropriateness. The substance of the attacks was typically meaningful, with the style of the attack providing a rhetorical obstacle. By questioning the motives and scholarly affiliations of the Jesus Seminar organization, the apologists succeeded in removing some of the Seminar's credibility. Also, by criticizing the voting method as an undemocratic publicity stunt, the traditionalists were able to cast their accusers as less than honorable. Perhaps the most damaging attacks were those brought against what the traditionalists saw as the Seminar's epistemological unfairness in undermining a supernaturalist worldview in favor of a naturalistic perspective. In addition, the attacks against the Seminar's effect on traditional faith likely were useful for influencing religious audiences. So the counterattacks were effective in marginalizing the Seminar to some extent and clarifying boundaries, but they were sometimes unnecessarily harsh, occasionally bordering on outright *ad hominem*. The strong invectives lobbed at the Seminar and its membership were likely useful for audiences that already share the general perspective of the traditionalists. Such "preaching to the choir" tactics were likely of little value, however, in converting the uncommitted or satisfying their accusers. The attacks against the traditionalists' accusers were somewhat well-conceived, but not always delivered with a broad audience in mind.

Next, Johnson's (1996) use of differentiation was useful as a prelude to the transcendence discourse, but not particularly significant or effective in itself. By claiming that traditional Christianity is concerned with faith, not history, Johnson departs from the traditionalist program of defense, and he contradicts most of his preceding arguments. He had already made a series of arguments concerning the record of history and methodological premises for establishing historical facts. Therefore, attempting to claim that traditionalists are doing something other than history was a significant incongruity in his position. However, with the shift to transcendence near the end of his discourse, this differentiation becomes useful.

As the final image restoration strategy, transcendence was a meaningful component of the traditionalists' response although the relationship between the transcendent rhetoric and the other *apologia* discourse is paradoxical. After denying the central accusations, attacking their accusers, and differentiating the nature of their supposed offense, the traditionalist apologists concluded with a form of evangelical appeal that resituates the issue in a larger, cosmic context. These instances of transcendence work to reframe the issue as something far more important than historical squabbles, and they are well-designed to reinforce the positions of their supporters, but they seem, at first glance, to run counter to the aims of the previous defenses. However, if the nature of the *apologia* is to answer the Seminar on all counts without ever accepting the presuppositions, or reality as defined by the Seminar, then it is not unreasonable to shift to transcendence. The traditionalists did not deny that the acts occurred, just that the acts did not occur as defined by the Seminar. If something was done, just not what the Seminar claimed was done, then some explanation is required. Johnson's (1996) differentiation provides the distinction, then the transcendent claims provide the broad explanation for how traditional Christian belief and practice reduces the offensiveness of the Seminar's attacks. If, indeed, these examples of transcendence are designed to answer the Seminar without accepting the reality of the Seminar, and in fact offering an alternative, then it is a sound decision.

With their various uses of denial, attack, differentiation, and transcendence, the traditional Christian apologists implemented a somewhat effective *apologia*. If there had been more effort to distinguish between character and policy issues, more shifting of the blame to televangelists and extreme conservatives, a pointed effort to bolster the academic credibility of traditionalists, and perhaps more clarity in the use of differentiation and transcendence to establish a distinction between the Seminar and traditionalism, this program of defense would have been more effective.

Next, it is important to assess the persuasive impact of the traditionalists' defenses. In doing so, it is important to consider the ambiguity of this enterprise. None of the apologists address a defined audience. There are vague references made that suggest they were aiming their discourse at an intellectually curious, but nonacademic popular audience. Clearly they were not addressing a purely scholarly audience, otherwise they would have published their defenses in journals. The fact that the defenses were contained in popular, mass-market books suggests that the intended audience was diverse and widespread.

With this in mind, it is tremendously difficult to evaluate the impact of these discourses on such an anonymous group. With the limited means available to measure rhetorical effect, it seems that the success of this *apologia* appears to be marginal. First, the works of prominent traditional Christian scholars have promoted an attention and opposition to the activities of the Jesus Seminar among traditional believers (Neary, 1998); however, this influence has been largely confined to audiences who were already predisposed to a traditional perspective.

Second, there are numerous books still being published concerning the Jesus of history and the Christ of faith; therefore the defense has been at least partly responsible for promoting an ongoing discussion and debate about the relationship between faith communities and a scientific study of history (see Crossan, 1998). It stands to reason that if members of the Jesus Seminar continue to publish apologetic discourses it must be in part a response to their opposition.

Third, the traditionalists' *apologia* seems to have had little impact in dissuading the efforts of the Jesus Seminar. The Seminar's web site contains information concerning the ongoing public meetings and organizational publishing. The traditionalists' discourse has not ended the Seminar's activity.

After considering the effects of the apologists' rhetoric on potential audiences, it seems that a final component of the assessment could be that the program of defense could have been far more successful if it had targeted specific audiences. Perhaps the absence of a defined audience grants rhetors the freedom of claiming persuasive effects wherever they might be found; however, the absence of such specificity does little to assist in the evaluation process of image restoration.

In terms of its internal logic and cogency, the *apologia* of traditional Christian apologists in response to the Jesus Seminar's attacks appears to be somewhat well-conceived and successful. However, this program of image restoration discourse could have been organized and communicated more effectively.

SUMMARY

In the quest for the historical Jesus, scholars have clearly lined up according to whether they see Jesus as a historical problem to be answered or as primarily an object of faith and worship. In response to the discourse of the Jesus Seminar, Christian apologists employed the image restoration strategies of denial, attacking accusers, differentiation, and transcendence. With their denials, the traditionalists partially deflected the charges of deception and ineptitude, even though they could have strengthened their denial if they had appropriately shifted the blame. By attacking their accusers, they established a clear distinction between themselves and the Jesus Seminar. The counterattacks further worked to reduce the offensiveness of the traditionalists by calling into question the credibility of their detractors. The differentiation and transcendence fold in together to accentuate the mysteries of God and faith that reach beyond the mundane context of scholarly disputes. While this program of defense could have been organized better, it was marginally successful.

As Christian *apologia*, this case recalls many of the discursive moves of the historical apologists, whose apologies were functioning at critical turning points in history. Perhaps time will someday reveal that the conflict in this chapter contained a defining moment in how Christian believers conceptualized the character of Jesus. As such momentous issues come to a point of crisis, the religious rhetors seem compelled to, among other things, draw distinctions between themselves and their opponents, and promote a culture of transcendence that casts the issue against a different backdrop. What is most interesting about this example is that it is the first in this current study to showcase the modern epistemological struggle between faith and science, or faith and naturalistic inquiry.

The rhetoric of this *apologia* continues to reinforce a protestant lineage by challenging the authority of anyone to interfere with the relationship between the individual and God. This is accomplished by a relatively unswerving commitment to the authority of scripture as a presumptive standard for epistemic interpretation, even when faced with scientific or historical evidence to the contrary.

NOTES

1. A recent search of LexisNexis databases located more than 200 references to the Jesus Seminar.

2. Opponents of the Jesus Seminar will be referred to as conservatives and traditionalists, which is not meant to imply that they are all conservative or traditional in every respect, nor does it suggest that they are uniform in their doctrines, faith practices, or even in their views of the historical Jesus. Conservatives and traditionalists are not found in only one sect; they are fundamentalists, evangelicals, Pentecostals, mainline Protestants, Catholics, and Orthodox believers. However, in reference to the typically liberal and revolutionary positions of the Jesus Seminar, they would generally stand together in opposition.

3. Occasionally, claims and discourse will be attributed to the Jesus Seminar as a whole. While the Seminar comprises the often diverse views of hundreds of scholars, they have chosen to publish their findings as a representation of the entire group; therefore when it is appropriate, general positions will be ascribed to the Jesus Seminar rather than attempting to ferret out the individual sources of data.

4. While the Seminar's later publication *The Acts of Jesus* (1998) contains further attacks against traditionalists, this study will only consider the earlier works by the Seminar to which responses have been directed.

5. With these claims the traditionalist position reflects the Pauline rhetoric recorded in I Corinthians 15:12–19 where the writer of the Corinthian epistle claims that if Christ was not crucified and resurrected, then faith is pointless and there is no hope.

6. Other scholarly rebuttals include arguments from Blomberg (1994), Craig (1995), Habermas (1995), Johnson (1996), McKnight (1995), Witherington (1997), and Yamauchi (1995).

7. This argument is also reflective of Pauline rhetoric in I Corinthians 1:20–27 where the writer distinguishes the wisdom of God and the wisdom of humanity.

6

Standing by Their Men: Southern Baptists and Women Scorned

In the wake of Southern Baptist Convention decisions in 1997 to boycott Disney, condemn homosexuality, and attack lesbian actress Ellen DeGeneres (Griffith & Harvey, 1998), the denomination's vote in 1998 to amend its statement of faith seemed somewhat mild. On June 9, 1998, representatives of the nearly sixteen million–member Southern Baptist Convention voted to amend the *Baptist Faith and Message* (1963) with a resolution on family and marriage roles that included the statement, "A wife is to submit herself graciously to the servant leadership of her husband, even as the church willingly submits to the headship of Christ." As expected, this move by the nation's largest Protestant denomination sparked a firestorm of media inquiry and public criticism.

Even though the amendment carries no enforcement power in a denomination that resists creedal compliance, the convention sent a message that was flatly resisted by opponents. The amendment is similar to the positions held by such groups as the Promise Keepers; however, the direct proclamation on wifely submission moved beyond the frequently ambiguous statements from other groups. The issue gathered enough public interest for the public television program,

"Religion and Ethics Weekly," to name the wifely submission amendment one of the top ten news stories of the year.

The issue is clearly significant. It has been widely reported in newspapers[1] and television news (Warner, 1998; Wehmeyer & Jennings, 1998). Under attack from feminists and moderate Baptists, conservative Southern Baptist women and men publicly defended the amendment on *Larry King Live* (1998) and CNN *Talkback Live* (Battista, 1998). The issue even received comment from such prominent Southern Baptists as former President Clinton and Vice President Gore ("Clinton disagrees," 1998).[2] The activities of Southern Baptists have managed to grab the attention of scholars as well.[3]

On June 9, 1998, delegates attending the Southern Baptist Convention's annual meeting in Salt Lake City adopted a resolution reinforcing a platform of traditional Christian family values. The statement, entitled "Article on the Family," was approved as an amendment to the 1998 *The Baptist Faith and Message* and sparked a great deal of public reaction. Within the text of the amendment, between statements defining marriage as exclusively heterosexual union and the importance of children obeying their parents, is found this statement:

> The husband and wife are of equal worth before God, since both are created in God's image. The marriage relationship models the way God relates to His people. A husband is to love his wife as Christ loved the church. He has the God-given responsibility to provide for, to protect, and to lead his family. A wife is to submit herself graciously to the servant leadership of her husband even as the church willingly submits to the headship of Christ. She, being in the image of God as is her husband and thus equal to him, has the God-given responsibility to respect her husband and to serve as his helper in managing the household and nurturing the next generation. (online)[4]

Although this amendment is a not a binding creed requiring obedience, the cultural implication of the sixteen million–member Southern Baptist Convention (SBC) declaration that women should "graciously submit" to their husbands provoked a tremendous amount of persuasive attack and defense.

Before analyzing the *kategoria* and *apologia* surrounding this issue, it is important to briefly consider the background of Southern Baptist conflict. First, the Southern Baptist Convention is perhaps the most democratically organized Protestant denomination, without formal hierarchies to dictate matters of belief or practice. Since the tradition has been for each church and individual to remain autonomous, the consequence has been that change often occurs only through severe rhetorical upheaval (Ammerman, 1990).

Second, recent SBC history reveals an ongoing tension between conservative and moderate factions. Farnsley (1994) observes that Southern Baptists have been particularly preoccupied with political struggles and boundary setting since the beginning of a fundamentalist takeover in 1979. In their eventually successful bid to seize control of leadership positions, fundamentalists have sought to purge the SBC of employees and professors who do not accept the belief that the Bible is literally true, without any errors, and should be interpreted uniformly. While this practice is difficult to reconcile with the democratic structure of the denomination, and significant resistance continues to exist in the convention, scholars such as Huebner (1991) and Stone (1992) continue to point to the power struggle surrounding biblical inerrancy as a defining characteristic of Southern Baptist discourse.

Third, fundamentalist SBC leaders continue to advance their theologically conservative agenda through denominational decrees. Since the mid-1980s, convention leaders have worked to remove individuals from Southern Baptist offices and seminaries who do not hold to the inerrantist position (see Ammerman, 1990; Barnhart, 1986; Farnsley, 1994; Huebner, 1991; Stone, 1992).[5] More recently, the convention has adopted resolutions publicly condemning homosexual culture, calling on Southern Baptists to boycott Disney for its condoning of homosexuality, and condemning actress Ellen DeGeneres for "coming out" as a gay character on national television. So the 1998 "Article on the Family" could be viewed as the next fundamentalist challenge, since it is the first amendment to the SBC's faith statement in more than 35 years (only the second since 1925), and it requires a literal, specific interpretation of such New Testament passages as Ephesians 5:22–24, which reads,

> Wives, submit to your husbands as to the Lord. For the husband is the head of the wife as Christ is the head of the church, his body, of which he is the Savior. Now as the church submits to Christ, so also wives should submit to their husbands in everything.[6]

By taking this position, the SBC aligns itself with such conservative religious organizations as Promise Keepers and Focus on the Family (see Griffith & Harvey, 1998), which promote male headship of the family, but who have not made the same sort of official proclamations. Regardless of the motives or intentions, Southern Baptists continue to use the leadership of the convention to shape an increasingly narrow ideology.

Fourth, these conflicts are rooted in a basic epistemological conflict, which influences the positions rhetors take and the way they communicate. Conservatives, who represent the dominant leadership in the SBC, tend to view the Bible as authoritative and unambiguous on all issues of faith and practice. Moderate and liberal dissenters generally accept the Bible as authoritative, but remain more open to interpretation than their counterparts. As a result, there is a great deal of rhetorical conflict.

ATTACKS AGAINST THE SOUTHERN BAPTIST CONVENTION

The "Article on the Family" quickly became known through the widespread media coverage as a Southern Baptist call for "wifely submission." As might be expected, this dimension of the amendment received a great deal of public attack from women's groups, fellow Southern Baptists, liberal Christian groups, and various other critics outside the denomination.

Although attacks against the Southern Baptists came from many sources, the focus of the attacks is generally limited to a few issues. Most of the accusations included reference to repeated offenses of hypocrisy in applying biblical teachings, a detrimental effect on male-female relationships, and the cultural impact this action would have on women and gender roles in society.

Many of the accusers attacked the SBC for flaws in their theology. Some opponents, such as Christian historian Martin Marty, characterize the amendment as primarily designed to reinforce the fundamentalists' doctrine of biblical inerrancy (Grossman, 1998). Others maintain that the SBC's statement on the family is inconsistent. Journalist and historian A. N. Wilson (1998) argues that if Southern Baptists are going to claim the inerrancy and authority of scripture in this case they must also tolerate slavery, promote communal living, poverty, and pacifism. He suggests a degree of hypocrisy when he writes, "Even the most ardent fundamentalists have to be highly selective in their fundamentals" (p. A31). In a similar tone, David Scholer, professor of New Testament at Fuller Theological Seminary, refers to the amendment as a case of "selective literalism" (Steinfels,

1998, p. A11), noting that the New Testament also calls believers to wash each others' feet, but only a few extreme Baptist groups practice such a teaching. The dean of Wake Forest University's Divinity School, Bill Leonard, strengthens this type of attack when he claims that the SBC statement on wifely submission uses the same sort of justification as earlier Baptists used to defend slavery, for which they just recently apologized. He questions, "I wonder if it will be another century before they apologize to women" (Vara & Holmes, 1998, p. A1). President of the National Organization for Women Patricia Ireland also points out the apparent contradiction in supporting this biblical distinction between men and women without supporting slavery when she states, "I think it's odd to be able to pull that out of the Bible and not pull with it the very closely—very close scriptural line that says slaves should submit to their masters" (King, 1998, p. 3).[7] These attacks establish that media representatives, religious scholars, and women's groups characterized the Southern Baptists' acts as offensive.

While the SBC's declaration was criticized on a theological level, it was also considered offensive due to its perceived implications concerning gender. Lois M. Powell, a Church of Christ minister, calls the declaration "a reaction and an affront to the social movement for women's rights" (Steinfels, 1998, A11). Maggie Harney, Episcopal priest and director of a women's center, attacks the dominance of patriarchal structures and their failures by stating, "It's so damaging to women's self-understanding, to their understanding about who they are before God" (Battista, 1998, p. 7). Robert Parham, executive director of the Baptist Center for Ethics, concurs: "I think they hope to make June Cleaver the biblical model for motherhood, ignoring the many biblical references about women who worked outside the home" (Battista, 1998, p. 4). He goes on to claim that "the statement reads as if husbands and wives should be more concerned about the lordship of the husband than the partnership of the couple" (Battista, 1998, p. 4). Carolyn Weatherford Crumpler, executive director of the Women's Missionary Union of the SBC, attacks the perception of exclusively female submission when she claims that the passage in Ephesians "is talking more about mutual submission in order for there to be unity and cooperative effort" (Warner, 1998, p. 2). This idea of unfair burdens of submission is continued by Dee Dee Myers, former White House press secretary, when she says that the amendment "implies that men need to take more responsibility, because women aren't necessarily up to it" (King, 1998, p. 24).

Patricia Ireland broadens the scope of the attack when she claims that the amendment

> raises some very important questions with real serious implications for our culture and religion is one of the institutions that shapes our culture and our views. And if this is now saying that we're putting the imprimatur of saying that God has ordained that men have a responsibility, an obligation to take leadership, and women have a re-sponsibility to take a step back and be subservient, I think that's a political message and it is something that we have to contend. (King, 1998, p. 8)

In a response that was significant in size and severity, this volley of accusations casts the SBC as culturally offensive to women and their desire for equality.

Finally, the SBC was presented as offensive in that this declaration is only one act in a history of offensiveness. Most of the attackers simply imply such a claim, but John Reed, a Southern Baptist pas-tor, suggests that such unfairness is a pattern of behavior for the SBC when he says, "This is not the first time Southern Baptists' funda-mentalist leaders have taken a position that demeans women" (King, 1998, p. 16). With the suggestion that the SBC has performed simi-lar acts of offense in the past, the attack grows in severity.

As the largest Protestant denomination in the United States, it is no surprise that the Southern Baptist Convention's "Article on the Family" prompted such a response. However, the extent of public criticism may have surprised the Baptist leadership. With the pro-nounced attack against it in place, the Southern Baptist Convention had sufficient motivation to defend its organizational image.

CRITICAL ANALYSIS OF THE SOUTHERN BAPTIST DEFENSE

Facing an onslaught of media commentary and criticism shortly after the ratification of the "Article on the Family," Southern Baptist representatives conducted press conferences and appeared on nation-ally televised talk shows in an effort to explain their positions and cleanse the denomination's public image. With special attention given to newspaper articles and television transcripts, this study finds that Southern Baptist defenders employ the strategies of denial, bolster-ing, attacking accusers, differentiation, and transcendence.

Denial

While nearly all of the defensive discourse is designed to reduce the offensiveness of the declaration, Paige Patterson, newly elected president of the Southern Baptist Convention and widely held to be the instigator of the fundamentalist takeover, argues in a press conference that the SBC has done nothing wrong. He suggests that there is no reason for offense when he states, "Frankly, I am a little surprised that anybody is surprised" (Vara & Holmes, 1998, p. A1). On behalf of the convention, he then claims there is no wrongdoing by denying that the amendment "is a negative statement against anybody or anything" (Scanlon, 1998, p. A1). In a similar denial of offensiveness, televangelist Jerry Falwell, himself affiliated with the SBC, argues that "nowhere in the amendment is there any suggestion of the husband being a dictator or overlording it" (King, 1998, p. 3). These denials are attempts to deflect the accusations initially; then, the apologists turn to more complex efforts to diminish the impact of the perceived offenses.

Bolstering

Southern Baptist apologists use bolstering to enhance their credibility as competent theologians and as fair people. While it is a minimal component of the defense, the few cases of bolstering are designed to justify the convention's position as less offensive than it might have first been viewed.

Albert Mohler, president of the Southern Baptist Seminary in Lousville, Kentucky, bolsters his image when his credibility as a Greek scholar is questioned. Mohler responds that he does read Greek, and is a competent translator (King, 1998, p. 19). Tom Elliff, who had just finished his term in 1998 as president of the SBC, bolsters the image of the group that wrote the "Article on the Family" when he says, "This committee is comprised of people who are great Bible scholars, both men and women" (Battista, 1998, p. 3). With this statement, Elliff promotes both the academic quality and the gender balance of the committee. However, it remains unclear if the women on the committee had equal power to change the amendment as the men, or if they were chosen for their predisposition to support such a statement.

Elliff goes on to provide support for the content of the amendment by claiming that the principles it contains are responsible for successful marriages. He claims that he has used these ideas in hundreds of cases of premarital counseling, and "only two that I know of in these 24 years of performing marriages have now ended in divorce" (Battista, 1998, p. 6). This claim bolsters the image of the amendment as useful in contributing to happy marriages.

Representing Southern Baptists as fair-minded, Anthony Jordan, the chairman of the resolution committee claims, "We're not trying to exclude anyone here" (Warner, 1998, p. 5). With a similar result in mind, some male defenders introduce personal narratives throughout their *apologia* about how much they respect their wives and how they are mutually submissive in their marriages.

These instances of bolstering are efforts to reduce the offensiveness of the amendment. By promoting the scholarship and the fairmindedness of Southern Baptists, these leaders hope to reposition themselves in the minds of their audience.

Attack Accusers

Southern Baptist defenders attack their accusers over issues of biblical interpretation. By casting their opponents as biblically illiterate, they hope to undermine the original accusations, which were based on interpretations of scripture.

One form of attack by the apologists was to claim that their opponents were not carefully reading scriptural text. In response to the perceived attack that the Southern Baptists' resolution included heated language, Paige Patterson replies, "It's only hot language to someone not real familiar with the Bible" (Kloehn, 1998, p. 1N). Albert Mohler, in response to a woman who claimed to have read the Bible backward and forward without seeing the doctrine the SBC was teaching, says, "If she's read it backwards and forwards she's evidently skipping a few pages here and there if she didn't find that!" (King, 1998, p. 17). In both of these cases, the apologists attack their accusers for imprecise understandings of biblical teaching.

More specifically, attacks are made against accusers for their interpretations of Greek. At issue is the use of the Greek verb *hupotasso*, which is the term for "submit" in the New Testament passages used to justify wifely submission. As part of the challenge against the SBC amendment, Catherine Kroeger, biblical studies professor at Gordon-Conwell Seminary, defines the term as "to associate with, to attach to, to ally with or relate with in a meaningful way" (Weiss, 1998, p. 1G). This interpretation drastically changes the meaning of submission and denies the hierarchical position of the amendment. Dorothy Patterson, co-author of the amendment and wife of SBC president Paige Patterson, attacks all such opposing scholars when she states, "They just say, 'This is the primary meaning' when it doesn't even make sense. The words have clear meanings. . . . The roots of *hupotasso*—'to place under'—aren't ambiguous" (Weiss, 1998, p. 1G). So, in an effort to indict her accusers for linguistic and hermeneutic incompetence, Dorothy Patterson seeks to promote the Southern Baptist interpretation. It is ironic that this move, along with attacking the accuser, also works to confirm the position that most accusers find so offensive.

These attacks, which strike at the character and policies of the accusers, are used by Southern Baptist apologists to reposition themselves as less offensive. The apparent desire is that by questioning the biblical authority of their opponents, the Southern Baptist position will be perceived as more acceptable.

DIFFERENTIATION

Various Southern Baptist supporters use differentiation to shift public understanding of the situation. Since most of their detractors view the resolution as an instrument of oppression, defenders work to draw a distinction between submission as domination and submission as part of a loving respectful relationship.

Tom Elliff distinguishes between a biblical model for submission and the type of submission that invites abuse when he says, "There are different kinds of submission. . . . This resolution is a statement of scripture and it's not calling for a wife to become a doormat for an uncaring husband" (Battista, 1998, p. 15). While he is not entirely specific about the types of submission, he demonstrates that a scriptural model is separate from the type of submission that allows the husband to take unfair advantage of his wife. The emphasis is on reducing the offensiveness of the amendment by suggesting that submission is something other than what the accusers say it is.

Elliff goes further, differentiating the resolution as an ideal principle rather than a requirement for daily practice. He compares the ideological influence of the amendment to that of the United States Constitution:

> It's a statement of ideal. There are people that violate the Constitution, but the Constitution is the ideal for the law of the land. We don't say, "Well, because people don't live that way, we're going to throw the Constitution out." (Battista, 1998, p. 7)

By making this argument, Elliff works to deflect the microscopic arguments about every conflict in the home. This response allows for more relaxed implementations of the declaration, thereby moving to reduce the offensiveness.

Transcendence

Southern Baptist apologists use transcendence more frequently than any other strategy in an effort to address the perceived offensiveness of the amendment. Attempting to move the issue into a broader context, Baptist defenders reduce offensiveness by concentrating on two primary issues: the breakdown of the American family and the authority of the Bible. Albert Mohler describes the transcendent tone of the defense when he says, "I can promise you that Southern Baptists knew that the culture at large would not understand necessarily what we were talking about, but we had hoped they would look at the larger context of this statement" (King, 1998, p. 8). The clear intention is to diminish the specific responses to the charges, and to transform perceptions of the situation.

First, the apologists defend the amendment as an attempt to preserve and rebuild the disintegrating family. Daniel Akin, dean of theology at the Southern Baptist Theological Seminary, sets the stage for this transcendent appeal when he describes the problem as "little boys and little girls growing up without a godly mother and a godly daddy to love, guide and nurture them" (Grossman, 1998, p. 6D). With reference to these problems of family life, Paige Patterson claims that the Southern Baptist declaration "is a statement that is made in a time of growing crisis in the family" (Vara & Holmes, 1998, p. A1). Anthony Jordan further supports the amendment as an impetus for positive change, describing it as "a clear call to biblical principles of family life" (Vara & Holmes, 1998, A1). In his answer to why the *Baptist Faith and Message* had not been amended in 35 years, Tom Elliff refers to the transcendent context by saying, "In 1963 the home wasn't under the kind of attack that it is under now" (Battista, 1998, p. 3). In each of these responses, the central argument seems to be that the problems of the American family justify the SBC's actions. Moreover, the transcendent tone and substance of such responses work to cast any opponent as an enemy of the family—a sacrosanct American institution.

In the next type of transcendent defense, the Southern Baptist rhetors appeal to the higher authority of God and the Bible. Tom Elliff supplies the rationale for this move:

> And so we felt like, while many other denominations seem to waffling about the roles of husband and wife, the sexual roles of men and women, we felt like it was important for us to go right back to the Bible, find what the Bible, which is always relevant to every society, every generation, we discovered what the Bible would say and simply state what God's word says. (Battista, 1998, p. 3)

This statement reveals the importance of obeying the Bible as the literal word of God. Albert Mohler assumes this authority when he says, "The statement comes right out of scripture" (King, 1998, p. 4). However, Mohler goes beyond mere rational authority, positioning the Bible—and apparently a single interpretation of it—as *de facto* authoritative, even if there are issues that are not entirely clear:

> There may be some things you and I can't understand yet, but we will understand one day and I will tell you this: there's not one jot or tittle of scripture that doesn't belong there, and I take that on the authority of the Lord himself. (King, 1998, p. 20)

This same sort of existential leap, transcending the context of the original accusations, is evident when Mary Mohler, co-author of the resolution and wife of Albert Mohler, says, "It doesn't take a scholar to be able to interpret what is clearly laid out in God's blueprint for the family." (Steinfels, 1998, p. A11). Such statements suggest that the offensiveness of the accusations will diminish if auditors will simply quit trying to intellectualize the issue and just position it against the unquestioned wisdom of God, which is unambiguously revealed in the Bible, and precisely communicated in the amendment. Mary Mohler recognizes that such a view of submission and scriptural authority may be unpopular, but when understood within the context of biblical truth, it is less offensive: "I do not do that because it's a command from Al Mohler. I do it because it's a command from God Almighty" (Scanlon, 1998, p. A1). These defenders accept biblical authority as sufficient and transcendent, as Anthony Jordan demonstrates: "Really the amendment was put forth as the basis that came solely out of the scripture. And so we're very comfortable with it, and it was overwhelmingly adopted" (Warner, 1998, p. 2). Finally, as an illustration of the defiant nature of the Southern Baptist transcendence, Albert Mohler responds to John Reed's attacks about the demeaning of women:

> His problem is not with me. It's not with the Southern Baptist Convention. It's with the Scripture. These verses came right out of Scripture. And if he has a problem with that he's going to have to take that up with a higher authority than any of the leaders of the Southern Baptist Convention. (King, 1998, p. 17)

This type of statement clearly moves the issue to some broader context than just the issue of wifely submission.

In summary, the Southern Baptist's use of transcendence focuses on the broad issues of the American family and the authority of the Bible as an effort to move the conflict to a larger context. Next, the effectiveness of this *apologia* will be considered.

EVALUATION OF THE SOUTHERN BAPTIST CONVENTION'S DISCOURSE

This program of *apologia* performed by Southern Baptist rhetors appears to have been successful with audiences who were predisposed to the SBC's position on moral and theological issues; however, the defense seemed to be generally unsuccessful for other audiences. To explain and support this assessment, this section will consider the appropriateness of the Southern Baptist apologists' strategies. Next, an evaluation of public reactions to the image restoration efforts will be discussed.

While a variety of strategies were employed, it is significant to note that the Southern Baptist apologists never demonstrated any sorrow or remorse for their acts; neither did they attempt to evade responsibility for them. They simply denied that the act was really offensive, and they attempted to further reduce the offensiveness of the amendment.

First, the denials by Paige Patterson and Jerry Falwell were ill-conceived as an initial strategy. By denying the offense, when whole choruses of opponents were publicly registering their disapproval, and when there was no means of escaping blame for the action, Patterson did little to promote the SBC's public image. Falwell's attempt to deny the offensiveness of the amendment involved little more than the suggestion that the amendment was not offensive because he is an expert and he did not find it offensive. This move suggests that both apologists were unaware of, naive about, or simply unconcerned with public reactions. Furthermore, this denial is indicative of the manner in which Patterson, Falwell, and their fellow apologists misanalyzed their audiences.

Second, the limited use of bolstering was a fitting rhetorical choice; however, it was poorly implemented. It would certainly seem useful for apologists in this situation to promote themselves as scholarly and committed to equality. It would be difficult to view the accused as offensive if they were effectively depicted as credible academics who were sympathetic to the problems of women. The failure in this case was once again in the apologists' misunderstanding of their audiences. The apologists underestimated how skeptical their opponents were of their credentials and the apologists' sincerity about their desire for equality. Moreover, the rhetors did not seem to grasp the extent to which they were viewed as misogynists; therefore, the efforts at bolstering seem to fall far short of the mark due to their brevity and failure to establish the SBC as caring about the issues important to women.

Third, the tactic of attacking the accusers is, again, an appropriate strategy, but it is used poorly. The apologists essentially attack their opponents for not reading scripture the way some Southern Baptists do. The circularity of this argument accomplishes little in the effort to portray their accusers as offensive. The only audiences that would accept such an attack are those who already accept the SBC position. It appears that the only Southern Baptist counterattack that is substantively effective as an attack is the quarrel over the Greek term for submission. The apologists seem to make a coherent argument that their accusers are manipulating biblical text toward their own ends; unfortunately, this only works to distance the Southern Baptists from their opponents even more. By winning this argument, the apologists are entrenching the idea that they believe women should be placed lower than men on a hierarchy, thereby negating earlier claims that they were not saying anything offensive and that they were people committed to equality. At bottom, the Southern Baptist apologists misdiagnose the problem as a matter of biblical interpretation, when the problem is actually epistemological. Arguments over religious texts cannot be won if the opponent does not agree on a way of knowing, or what constitutes reliable knowledge and moral truth. Although the denial of offensiveness, bolstering, and attacking accusers dovetail nicely with their use of transcendence, the actual execution of the defenses was far less than effective.

Fourth, the use of differentiation is appropriate and employed fairly well. In the face of charges that they were promoting abusive, domineering leadership by men and weak acceptance by women, it was important for the defenders to draw a distinction between the accusations and what they were actually advocating. Some apologists did this, but they could have included more instances of differentiation and more specificity in defining their actual positions. Furthermore, Tom Elliff's statement comparing the amendment to the Constitution was effective as a strategy to reduce the offensiveness of the act. However, the move away from a strict treatment of submission as a function of a patriarchal hierarchy is to leave a great deal of room for interpretation. The dilemma for the apologists is they have either a policy that is reprehensible to their opponents, or they have a policy that does nothing and is unsatisfactory to their supporters. So the use of differentiation serves to diminish the impact of the original attack by weakening the central SBC position.

The final strategy of transcendence is the most significant and well-implemented of the Southern Baptists' image repair efforts. While this rhetorical approach still reveals a profound inability on the part of the SBC apologists to analyze opposing audiences, this form of *apologia* works to build support among various conservative Christian groups. By placing the issue in the wider contexts of family and the Bible, the apologists seem to effectively portray the issue as much larger than the particular squabbles over submission. The retreat to the strongholds of traditional family values and biblical authority promises to divert attention away from the charges and vilify any who oppose them, thereby reducing the offensiveness of the SBC's stance on the submission of women. However, the apologists fail to use this strategy to their advantage. They offer transcendent arguments with such an air of defiance and rigidity that the needs of families and the reverence for God's authority are eclipsed by the political agenda and arrogant rhetoric of the Southern Baptist representatives.

With some exceptions, the Southern Baptist program of defense incorporated appropriate strategies that were poorly executed. Given public sentiment, Patterson's denial may have severely undermined this program of defense. However, the tactics of denial of offensiveness, bolstering, attack, differentiation, and transcendence promised to answer the accusations and lessen the impact of the offense. Theoretically, the apologists could have denied offensiveness by showing expert evidence that the biblical notion of submission was not what their accusers said it was. They could have bolstered themselves better by clearly promoting their academic credentials and their desire for gender empowerment and equality. They could have cast their opponents as ill-equipped at biblical translation and interpretation. They could have elaborated their denials into actual differentiation by clearly stating what submission was if it was not what their opponents said it was. And, of course, they could have used mortification and corrective action in admitting they were misguided and changing the proclamation to be more gender inclusive; but that would have been an extremely unlikely scenario. These strategic failures, mixed with their lack of appropriate audience analysis and adaptation, hampered these devices from accomplishing much image restoration.

The external evidence suggests that the Southern Baptist apologists were tremendously successful in building support among those who share their specific political and theological beliefs and practices. They were not particularly successful, however, among their opponents.

There is evidence that the defense was successful among conservative evangelical audiences. Six weeks after the SBC vote on the amendment, the Southern Baptist Convention released a statement (Toalston, 1998) which indicated that more than 150 evangelical leaders communicated their public support for the Southern Baptist stance on marriage and the family. Contacted by Dennis Rainey, executive director of the FamilyLife ministry division of Campus Crusade for Christ, this group of Christian leaders agreed to sign a statement that they affirmed the SBC's position on the family. The list of names appeared in a full-page advertisement in *USA Today*,[8] and included such people as Chuck Colson, former counsel to President Nixon and chairman of Prison Fellowship; James Dobson, president of Focus on the Family; Bill McCartney, chairman of Promise Keepers; and numerous other influential figures in evangelicalism. Only two unnamed evangelical leaders refused to sign the list. While it would not be accurate to suggest that such a show of support resulted directly from the *apologia*, it would be fair to say that the image restoration efforts of the Southern Baptist apologists promoted such a move among audiences that were sympathetic to their doctrinal and political platforms.

There seem to be two possible reasons for this support. First, it is conceivable that these evangelical leaders and audiences were completely unaffected by the image restoration efforts, responding only to the public controversy. In fact, it could be argued that they threw their names into the battle because of perceived failures on the part of SBC apologists that prompted them to come to the rescue of this conservative evangelical cause. Second, the defenses may have been more effective with these audiences because their burden of proof, or threshold of resistance was considerably lower than their counterparts. Perhaps, if they are predisposed to the SBC position, they were more likely to supply their own support for arguments. For instance, when the claim was made that men were not dictators—but there was no alternate description of what they should be viewed as—it is possible that sympathetic audiences supplied the missing description, similar to the supplying of missing premise in an enthymeme. Either reason would account for conservative evangelical support for the SBC *apologia*, even in the face of poorly constructed and delivered defenses.

Responses from SBC opponents were equally strong in disagreement. Most notably, members of the Cooperative Baptist Fellowship, which is a breakaway group from the SBC, remained critical of the SBC after the initial conflict. Most of the respondents cited misinterpretation of scripture and negative attitudes as the problems with the Southern Baptist defense.[9] With similar results, an electronic poll conducted by *Women's Wire*, as a follow-up to the SBC action, found that with 3,889 responses, 78% of those voting thought wives should not submit to their husbands. Furthermore, a review of the personal comments suggests that the opposition to the SBC's statement was unaffected by the *apologia*, with most people holding to previous beliefs.

Similar to the reasons the evangelical audiences accepted the *apologia*, the opposing audiences may have rejected it for two reasons. First, they might have been so violently opposed to such a cultural perspective that they would have opposed it regardless of the quality of the defense. Second, the burden of proof for SBC apologists might have been so tremendously high with the opposition that anything short of a flawless public argument would have failed to satisfy them.

This examination suggests that the Southern Baptist apologists' effectiveness in restoring the image of the convention depends on the audience. The *apologia* seems to have failed with the popular media and general public. However, the image repair efforts were somewhat of a success among audiences who accepted the essential moral and biblical premises of the rhetors. What this evaluation demonstrates is that the foundational epistemic conflict that has prevented meaningful communication through and within the SBC for years continues to inhibit effective discourse.

SUMMARY

As the largest of American Protestant groups, advocates for the Southern Baptist Convention engaged in a protestantic defense of the denomination's public image. They used the strategies of denial, bolstering, attacking accusers, differentiation, and transcendence. The denials of offensiveness, in the face of a public that was so clearly offended, did not work to lessen the impact of the accusations against the SBC. By promoting their credentials and what they defined as fair treatment of women, the accused attempted to bolster their image. Southern Baptist representatives attacked their opponents vehemently. They differentiated their views of gender roles from the charges of misogyny they were facing. And, they transcended the issue, claiming that they were being obedient to the word of God and protecting the future of the family. While the tactics seem to be well-chosen, for the most part, the manner in which they were communicated was less than effective. In fact, this *apologia* was only successful with audiences that happened to already share the assumptions of these Southern Baptist apologists. This result suggests that at the bottom of some religious disputes are epistemological differences that must be addressed for an *apologia* to be successful.

As a comment on these three contemporary cases, I will make a few brief observations. Where the historical apologists shared a certain uniformity in content and style, the contemporary apologists were somewhat less so. They had many strategies in common, but their efforts were shot from very different trajectories. The traditionalists responding to the Jesus Seminar and the Southern Baptist apologists all faced challenges over their views of scripture and doctrine. They used denials, attacks, differentiation, and transcendence; moreover, both groups at least hinted at a form of bolstering. This image repair style seems to be fairly well-designed, at least in principle, for addressing conflicts over matters of truth and the spirit. Swaggart represented a different approach altogether. However, his case was unique in that it was not related to a defense of policy, it was purely a defense of character. Furthermore, it was a defense of character with unambiguous evidence that the accused was, in fact, culpable. As stated above, if he had stopped with his early defense, it could have served as a model for Christian *apologia* in such circumstances. All in all, the analysis of these three apologists assists in beginning to define a Christian *apologia*, and ultimately a sense of Christian rhetoric.

NOTES

1. A recent search of LexisNexis databases located more than 100 references to the controversy over wifely submission in the Southern Baptist Convention.

2. Other prominent Southern Baptists at the time included former House Speaker Newt Gingrich; Senate Majority Leader Trent Lott; House Majority Leader Tom DeLay; and House Minority Leader Richard Gephardt.

3. As an issue that carries serious cultural impact for gender relations in religion, the Southern Baptist resolution on wifely submission, and the subsequent defense of the resolution by convention representatives, is deserving of scholarly attention. There have been a fair number of studies concerning Southern Baptist controversies (Ammerman, 1990; Barnhart, 1986; Draper, 1984; Farnsley, 1994; Wiles, 1992), but few communication studies have examined Southern Baptist rhetoric or *apologia*. Huebner (1991) analyzed the rhetoric of heresy and orthodoxy as the doctrinal conflicts within the convention resulted in internal deviance and institutional redefinition. Stone (1992) also considered Southern Baptist struggles over biblical authority by examining how the social drama in the denomination has transferred power and reshaped members' perceptions.

4. The full text of the resolution can be found at http://www.sbc.net/bfm18.cfm.

5. A dramatic treatment of "the purge" can be found in the critically acclaimed documentary *Battle for the Minds* (Lipscomb, 1996), in which the dismissal of Dr. Molly Marshall from the Southern Baptist Seminary in Louisville, Kentucky is depicted as a manifestation of the fundamentalist takeover and the fundamentalists' intolerance of dissenting theologies and women in leadership.

6. For an extended treatment of the scriptural references and theological support for the statements in the amendment, see the *Report of Committee on Baptist Faith and Message* (1998).

7. The passage regularly referred to as the justification for slavery is Ephesians 6:5–8, which reads:

> Slaves, obey your earthly masters with respect and fear, and with sincerity of heart, just as you would obey Christ. Obey them not only to win their favor when their eye is on you, but like slaves of Christ, doing the will of

God from your heart. Serve wholeheartedly, as if you were serving the Lord, not men, because you know that the Lord will reward everyone for whatever good he does, whether he is slave or free.

8. A copy of the ad, entitled, "Southern Baptists . . . you are right!," is available at: http://www.youareright.org/usatoday_ad.htm.

9. Copies of these responses by members of the Cooperative Baptist Fellowship can be found at: http://www.cbfonline.org/viewpoint/sbc/responses.html.

Part III

Interpretations

7

Implications for Religious Rhetoric

I began with the general purpose of examining how image restoration theory applies to select examples of historical and contemporary religious discourse. In this chapter, the results of the critical applications will be discussed, with special attention given to the implications this research has on the development of Christian *apologia*. I will review the rhetorical strategies in each case as to their implementations and effects. I will then discuss the impacts these discoveries might have on the study and practice of religious rhetoric.

STRATEGIES

In an effort to funnel the results of each case into some manageable form, this section will summarize the strategies and assessment of each *apologia*. Then, the effect of the various contexts of the defenses will be considered.

Paul's *Apologia*

In the Apostle Paul's first-century defense of himself and his ministry, he utilized the strategies of bolstering, attacking accusers, and transcendence. He bolstered himself as an authentic apostle by claiming that his ministry was a result of divine appointment, that he had received the approval of church leaders, and by demonstrating that he was personally committed to the Galatians and to his faith. He attacked his accusers for denying the liberating message of grace by embracing the legalistic policy of circumcision, and for following selfish motives. Through his use of transcendence, he directed attention away from his character and focused on the broader issues of God's love, immutable truth, and the unification of Jewish and Gentile believers.

Paul's discourse was effective in deflecting the attacks and maintaining his standing as a leader and teacher in early Christendom; presumably this includes the believers at Galatia. By establishing that he was credible, that his accusers were not, and that his message was a matter of ultimate truth, he developed a consistent message of defense. His enduring influence in the works of theologians and moral philosophers further testifies to the persuasive value of his discourse.

Justin's *Apologia*

In his responses to the increasingly intense public persecutions of Christian believers, Justin employed the strategies of denial, bolstering, attacking accusers, and transcendence. He denied charges that believers were atheistic, sexually immoral, or responsible for the general ills of society. He bolstered the image of Christians by claiming that their beliefs were philosophically superior to opposing forms of paganism, and by associating Christians with acts of social charity and benevolent spiritual power. In heated counterattacks against the persecutors of Christians, Justin charged that they were overtly malicious and logically inconsistent in their public accusations and actions. With the use of transcendence, his most prevalent strategy, Justin submitted a vision of reality in which oppression, punishment, and even death diminished in importance when considered against the backdrop of God's will and eternity.

In spite of the fact that Justin was eventually martyred for his faith and discourse, his broad impact and transcendent goals worked to make this a generally effective case of defensive rhetoric. He could have strengthened the defense with a more specific denial, some appropriate blame-shifting, and a clearer differentiation between the offenses Christians were charged with and the nature of true Christian beliefs and practices; however, the tactics that were used were essentially consistent and complementary. Justin Martyr's *apologia* failed to sufficiently persuade his contemporary accusers to immediately cease the public persecutions of early believers, but it survived as an influence in early Christian discourse and as a model for Christian apology.

Luther's *Apologia*

The image restoration of Martin Luther at Worms occurred through two distinct phases of denial and transcendence. First, Luther denied the charges by focusing on the offensiveness of his acts. He made no attempt to deny that he had performed the alleged offenses. He simply denied that his actions were heretical. Second, he shifted the essential meaning of his trial away from his wrongdoings to the transcendent authority of scripture and individual conscience.

Luther's defense of himself was an appropriate use of image restoration discourse, and it was persuasive with an important portion of his audience. By focusing exclusively on the denial of offensiveness and transcendence, he worked to confront and challenge the predominant religious reality of his day. With his apology, he reshaped the meaning of what it meant to be spiritually offensive. While the arbitrating audience of officials did not accept Luther's defense, the German people seemed to embrace his discourse as a meaningful restoration of his personal image, as well as a rhetorical impetus for social and religious reform. Again, this case has survived as a model of Christian *apologia*, at least within the protestant lineage.

Swaggart's *Apologia*

Jimmy Swaggart, confronted with a much different accusation than the previous historical cases, used the strategies of mortification, bolstering, defeasibility, minimization, attacking accusers, and differentiation. His most meaningful public effort was his mortification, in which he openly acknowledged his sins and asked for forgiveness. He bolstered his image by appealing to the prevailing ethos of Protestant Pentecostalism and by associating himself with biblical figures. As his program of defense progressed, he argued defeasibility by claiming that his fatigue and longtime addictions had played a part in his actions. He also attempted to reduce the offensiveness of his acts by attacking his accusers, casting them as hypocrites out to destroy him out of jealousy. And he attempted to differentiate his actual behaviors from public charges of adultery.

This defense was ultimately ill-conceived and unpersuasive with the general public. The first phase of the *apologia*, which primarily focused on the acceptance of guilt and the act of repentance, lost its positive impact as Swaggart began to evade responsibility and reduce the offensiveness of his acts. As his excuses and justifications began to interfere with the sincere initial apology, his effectiveness diminished. This failure at maintaining the appearance of contrition combined with his unwillingness to be specific and forthright about the actual offense made for a poorly designed defense. This was further manifested in his subsequent financial and media losses, which relegated him to the position of a minor television evangelist.

Jesus Seminar Opponents' *Apologia*

The rhetorical attacks of the Jesus Seminar against traditional Christian beliefs and practices prompted traditionalist apologists to respond with denials, attacks against the accusers, differentiation, and transcendence. They denied that traditional Christian leaders were inept and deceptive. They launched a tremendous amount of counterattacks at the Jesus Seminar, questioning the motives of the Seminar, the academic credibility of the membership, and its research methodologies. Moreover, the apologists generally accused the Seminar of corrupting religious truth by bifurcating history and faith, thus undermining the deity and spiritual importance of Jesus. Some traditionalists differentiated between the practice of history and the practice of faith, claiming that the Seminar's attacks were diminished when it was understood that traditional Christianity was not primarily about history, but faith. The apologists ultimately transcended the issues by appealing to the desire to transform humanity by reconciling people with God.

This *apologia* was fairly well-designed, but only marginally persuasive. The image restoration strategy choices were meaningful, but the overall cogency of the apology was harmed by the lack of distinctions between character and policy issues. By failing to separate many of the *apologia* claims from the traditional apologetics, the image issues were often not isolated and impacted as separate from the philosophical and theological disputes. The apologists also failed to shift the appropriate amount of blame to the more fundamentalist members of Christian leadership and media. Furthermore, the epistemological differences were not as prominently displayed through differentiation and transcendence. The *apologia* was apparently less than effective in restoring the image of traditional Christianity for the Jesus Seminar. However, if part of the objective was to promote ongoing public discourse on the subject of the historical Jesus and traditional Christian faith, this case of image restoration rhetoric seemed to achieve that goal.

Southern Baptists' *Apologia*

In response to public condemnations for their 1998 statement on the family, which included the doctrine of wifely submission, Southern Baptist apologists used the image restoration strategies of denial, bolstering, attacking accusers, differentiation, and transcendence. Apologists denied that the Southern Baptist Convention's actions were offensive, claiming that the SBC was not advocating anything negative or oppressive. They bolstered Southern Baptists as scholarly and fair-minded. Attacks were launched against their accusers, suggesting that the opponents of the SBC were not competent at biblical interpretation and spiritual understanding. The apologists differentiated their notion of loving, mutually supportive submission from their opponents' views of submission as oppressive. Ultimately, they transcended the issue by appealing to the health of the American family and the infallible authority of God's word as revealed in the Bible.

These strategies appear to have been chosen well; however, they were executed poorly, resulting in a defense that was limited in its persuasiveness. On the whole, Southern Baptist apologists failed to analyze their audience. Denying the offensiveness of the amendment, when it was so obviously offensive to the public, was foolhardy. Bolstering their scholarly credentials without promoting their true interests in the concerns of women failed to ring true with a general audience. Also, failing to make it completely clear in their differentiations what submission was, if not oppressive, did not make the public case for a Southern Baptist defense. The use of transcendence was well-conceived, but delivered with such defiance that it lost much of its impact. The result was a defense that was effective with those who already supported their doctrine on the family. Those who opposed the SBC were generally unaffected by the *apologia*.

These chapter reviews indicate that Christian discourse is not always well-designed or persuasive; however, the rhetorical defenses in these six cases all contained some effective use of the available strategies. The most common image restoration strategies were transcendence and attacks against accusers, with five of the six cases using at least one of the two. Four cases used both strategies, and they made up the bulk of the discourse when they were part of the defense. The second most common strategies were denials and bolstering, each being used four times, with two cases containing both. It is also interesting to note that denial and transcendence were coupled on four occasions. Next in frequency was differentiation, with three instances. Defeasibility, minimization, and mortification were each used only once in all six cases. The image restoration strategies used in the six cases are reviewed in Table 7.1.

While eight different strategies were employed, repeated usage and focus were limited to only a few. Only the five strategies of denial, bolstering, attacking accusers, differentiation, and transcendence were used more than once.

The most notable differences in the various strategies used by the different apologists are found in the discourse of Luther and Swaggart. Luther was the only one of the six cases that did not attack his accusers. It is likely that he made the choice not to attack since his accusers were present before him, and they were one of his primary audiences. While the other apologists may have had occasion to encounter their attackers at some point, Luther was the only one who was facing his auditors while making his defense. In all the other cases, the defenses were made through written discourse or mass-media channels. Granted, the Southern Baptist apologists spoke with immediacy to present opponents, but they were not answering pointed accusations like Luther, nor were they standing alone. The effect of the group *apologia* may have emboldened them to speak up against their foes. Moreover, their attackers were not necessarily the audience they were concerned with.

Swaggart's defense was quite different from all the rest. He was the only apologist who did not use transcendence; furthermore, he was the only one to use minimization and mortification. Undoubtedly, the reason for these differences is that Swaggart was the only one of the six who believed himself to be—at least in part—in violation of a sacred belief or principle. As a result, he felt the need to acknowledge his guilt and seek forgiveness. This also discouraged him from appealing to some higher standards, like his transcendent counterparts.

Table 7.1
Image Restoration Strategies
Used by Christian Apologists

Historical Apologists

Apostle Paul
    bolstering
    attacking accusers
    transcendence

Justin Martyr
    denial
    bolstering
    attacking accusers
    transcendence

Martin Luther
    denial
    transcendence

Contemporary Apologists

Jimmy Swaggart
    defeasibility
    bolstering
    minimization
    attacking accusers
    differentiation
    mortification

Jesus Seminar Opponents
    denial
    attacking accusers
    differentiation
    transcendence

Southern Baptists
    denial
    bolstering
    attack accusers
    differentiation
    transcendence

Also, his use of minimization seems to be aimed at lessening the damage of acts he knew to be offensive rather than attempting to significantly reshape the reality of the situation.

The rhetorical choices in these six instances reveal some patterns and raise some interesting questions about image restoration. The importance of these strategy choices and their impact on Christian image restoration discourse will be discussed next.

THE EFFECTS OF CONTEXT

This section details the effect context had on the image restoration strategies used. First, the context of substance is considered as the strategies used to defend policies are compared to the strategies used to defend character. Second, the context of time is considered through a comparison of the historical examples and the contemporary defenses.

Policy Defenses and Character Defenses

Creating a clear delineation between defenses of policy and character is problematic. The objects of this study confirmed Benoit's (1995a) claim that "it is not easy to disentangle character from policy or to neatly separate defenses of character from defenses of policy" (p. 90). In fact, it was often so unclear as to where policy left off and character began that Ryan's (1982) claim—that policy or character would typically dominate the rhetoric—was only partially evident. For instance, Justin found himself defending the character of second-century Christians, but in doing so he was also defending their beliefs and doctrines. Southern Baptist apologists were often defending the policies of their convention, but in order to do so they were frequently addressing their character as ethical people. Therefore, determining the contextual influence of policy and character on the choices and effectiveness of image restoration strategies was troublesome. All the cases examined here were considered to be examples of *apologia*, due to the ultimate impact on the public image of the accused. However, the unique blend of apologetics and *apologia* in the discourse of the rhetors caused the blurring of boundaries.

As a means toward creating some manageable categories for evaluation, the cases are organized in terms of their focus. They are separated in the following way: primarily policy defenses, policy/character defenses that were dominated by policy considerations, character/policy defenses that were dominated by character considerations, and primarily character defenses.

The defenses that were predominantly policy issues included those by Paul and Luther. Paul was essentially defending the doctrine of grace, and Luther was defending a whole collection of theological principles ranging from grace to biblical authority. Interestingly, they were both historical instances that focused on either the denial of offensiveness or reducing offensiveness and they both utilized the specific strategy of transcendence. Furthermore, both defenses were well-conceived and generally held to be successful with their most salient audiences.

The opponents of the Jesus Seminar and the Southern Baptists represented the policy/character defenses. The traditionalists mostly defended their specific doctrines and beliefs, with some treatment of their ethical standing; the Southern Baptists were defending their amendment on the family, as well as addressing the way the public viewed them as people. Both defenses were performed by groups of apologists, they were both contemporary examples, and they used the same specific strategies, with the exception of the Southern Baptists' use of bolstering. Both defenders engaged in some denial, but mostly they reduced offensiveness through attacks against their accusers and transcendence. It is also interesting to note that both examples, while internally consistent in their choices of strategies, were generally ineffective in persuading the general public, perhaps because the apologists did not adequately address policy and character issues separately.

Justin supplied a character/policy defense. While he defended those who had adopted the beliefs and practices of Christianity, most of those public charges came in the form of moral, ethical accusations that undermined the character of the believers. His *apologia* differed from the more policy-oriented defenses in its use of more tacit denials. Also, he was unpersuasive with his immediate audience, his rhetorical success being found in his transcendent goals.

Clearly, Swaggart was the single case of a defense dominated by character issues. His *apologia* differed from all the others in that he attempted to evade responsibility, he minimized his offense, and he engaged in mortification. Furthermore, his defense was largely inconsistent and ineffective, not simply because it was a character defense, but because he failed to maintain a consistent, repentant appeal for forgiveness.

While the results are not stark in their distinctions, and the analysis of this issue was hindered by the trouble in distinguishing between policy and character defenses, the findings reveal some differences in policy and character defenses. However, it is difficult to determine if the differences in strategies are evidence of the effect of policy and character defenses, or if there are other intervening variables. It could be argued that a defense of policy is less likely to involve an evasion of responsibility or acceptance of blame, since policy-oriented defenses in this study mostly involved denials of offensiveness and reduction of offensiveness. It stands to reason that policy defenders would primarily focus their efforts on the offense (policy) itself, rather than on issues of responsibility; moreover, it is reasonable that character defenders would focus on accepting or avoiding blame (tacit denials, evasions of responsibility, mortification), since character issues focus more on culpability than the nature of the offense (policy). While this is a reasonable construal of the results, it is difficult to infer that policy and character contexts are the cause of these differences.

Finally, this study is a clear refutation of Kruse's (1981b) position that policy issues are not part of *apologia*. These findings demonstrate that policies can be inextricably tied to the character of an individual or group; therefore, defenses of policy can be significant parts of image repair discourse.

Historical and Contemporary Contexts

Except for the significant amount of contrast between the character defense of Jimmy Swaggart and the policy defenses of Paul and Martin Luther, there appears to be little difference between the historical cases and the contemporary cases. Swaggart's *apologia* was distinct in that he used three strategies (defeasibility, minimization, and mortification) that none of the other rhetors used, but the fact that he used quite different strategies than the other two contemporary examples suggests that the differences were not a result of historical position. That exception being taken into account, there is little deviation in the strategies from historical defenses to contemporary defenses.

However, it should be noted that all three of the contemporary rhetors used differentiation, and no differentiation was used in the historical discourse. Since differentiation involves asking an audience to see an event as something other than what they originally thought it to be, it seems to be implied that people do not share a universal vision of reality. Perhaps this is a uniquely contemporary concern. Wood (1998) suggests that problems in ancient epistemology centered around correctly apprehending or acting on the accepted divine design. This worldview presumed that reality was generally a shared experience and things were as they seemed to be. Wood goes on to characterize modern and postmodern epistemological concerns as being much more complex, revealing a view of reality that is far more fragmented and interpreted. Therefore, it seems that modern apologists would be more likely to seek to differentiate between competing realities than their historical counterparts.

Although the historical apologists seem to be advocating new realities with their use of transcendence, perhaps the attempt to expand and broaden the realities of their audiences (who were operating within a God-centered universe) is not asking as much of the audience as differentiation. Differentiation asks audiences to replace one reality with another, rather than expanding a reality into another.

It does seem possible that the evolution of epistemology could account for the appearance of differentiation in the modern cases of *apologia*. For the most part, the image restoration of these Christian rhetors seems to be rather unified: it does not seem to be affected by the passage of time.

CHRISTIAN *APOLOGIA*

Until this study, *apologia*, when applied to Christian discourse, was considered synonymous with apologetics, or theological defenses. Image discourse was rarely considered, except as it related to the development of theology. This study expands and divides the concept of apologetics to include the unique examination of image issues. Many of the findings and implications in this study coalesce to contribute to the development of a theoretical approach to Christian *apologia*.

Antecedent Constraints

Jamieson (1973a, 1973b) maintains that rhetorical responses to situations are strongly influenced by antecedent rhetorical forms. She argues that rhetors who feel strongly bound to tradition "feel generic constraints more acutely than does the rhetor not tied to a tradition-bound institution" (1973b, p. 165). Because religion is generally held to be the most ritualistic, tradition-bound institution in public life, it seems reasonable to expect that religious rhetors would be tremendously constrained by antecedent rhetorical forms.

This study seems to confirm this principle. All of the apologists considered here were either instrumental in forming biblical authority, exhibited a belief in the authority of biblical text, or made arguments that were directly reflective of biblical texts or church history, as is indicative of the protestant lineage. Since the force of traditional Christian preaching, central New Testament texts like the *Acts of the Apostles*, and the research of Blaney and Benoit (1997) strongly suggest that the dominant image restoration strategy in the New Testament is transcendence, it is only appropriate that Christian apologists would rely on transcendence as heavily as these did. Furthermore, since biblical text and teaching and the ethos of Protestant tradition all direct one to repent and seek forgiveness when cognizant of wrongdoing, it is consistent that the most successful strategy in Swaggart's defense was mortification.

Where political apologists might consider what is consistent with their party's present platform, or a corporation might consider what is consistent with current marketing strategies or legal precedent in avoiding liability, religious rhetors seem to be motivated more by their rhetorical tradition. The influence of biblical authority, church history, and "rhetorical saints" seem to exercise strong control over the discourse of Christian apologists, suggesting that antecedent genre constraints play a significant role in the formation of Christian *apologia*.

Role of Epistemology

Another implication for religious image restoration discourse is the role epistemology plays in the understanding of attacks and construction of defenses. In this study, the attacks and defenses were as often about how individuals and groups come to know as they were about public behaviors.

With Swaggart as the sole exception, each of the cases in this study seemed to be as much about the epistemic activities of the accused as the public manifestations of those activities. Paul was attacked for rejecting Judaic law and ritual as spiritual "knowing." Justin and the early Christians were, in part, attacked for their peculiar cosmology. Luther was fundamentally accused of violating the ontological and epistemological authority of the church. The traditionalist apologists were criticized for how they came to know their faith. The Southern Baptists were essentially attacked for the way they construct knowledge of spiritual and ethical truths. In each case, the conflict is not so much over the actions of the accused, but their defiance of some form of epistemological status quo.

This is particularly significant given the previous discussion of the blurring of policy and character defenses. As attacks and defenses center more on the knowing of the accuser and the accused, it becomes increasingly difficult to distinguish between the nature of the person and the contents of their beliefs and principles. It seems that the epistemology of an individual or a group is at the very nexus between character and policy. The way a person or group knows is at the heart of their identity and ethical character, but it also is the foundational essence for their behaviors and principles.

So perhaps epistemology is the bridge between character and policy. As a thin membrane through which thought is transposed into action, the way of knowing seems to explain the fusion of, or at least confusion between, policy and character.

The influence of epistemology in *apologia* helps explain the difficulties experienced in some Christian image repair. Through their uses of transcendence, often invoking entrenched worldviews, some of the Christian apologists in this study ended up with such totalizing and polarizing rhetoric that little room was left for any discursive negotiation. While that may often be the intent of religious discourse—not seeking to meet the standards of this world—considering the impact of epistemology in the rhetoric of *apologia* contributes to an understanding of what Weaver (1970) meant when he declared that "language is sermonic" and that our utterances give "impulse to other people to look at the world, or some small part of it, in our way" (p. 224). Grant (1988) illuminates this prospect when he writes,

> An apologist who finds the link in philosophy or cultural life will lay emphasis on aspects of philosophy or culture that favor his own group's attitudes and ideals and, at the same time, will emphasize a philosophical or cultural analysis or structuring of his group's views. (p. 9)

If apologists conceive of themselves as more than just defenders of character and policy, but as epistemological agents or advocates, they may become more effective at restoring their public image.

Strategies

Beyond the strategic implications discussed earlier, it is appropriate to note that there are some strategies that appear to be uniquely useful in Christian *apologia*. Primarily, the important tactics for Christian apologists are transcendence and mortification, with bolstering and attacking accusers playing fairly significant roles as well. There are also minor strategies that are supportive of these.

As Blaney and Benoit (1997) contended, transcendence did emerge in this study as the most prominent strategy for Christian apologists. Paul, Justin, and Luther were all generally considered successful in their defenses, and they all made generous use of transcendence. Moreover, the more successful portions of the Jesus Seminar opponents' and the Southern Baptists' defenses seemed to be in their uses of transcendence. Denial of additional charges, shifting blame, and denial of offensiveness could be used as complementary strategies within a transcendent framework. By focusing on the truth or the severity of the offense, they could be used effectively to cleanse the religious image.

While it is not always used persuasively, transcendence has been shown to be a signature of Christian *apologia*. Transcendence is a mark of Christian *apologia* that is designed to defend a theological principle, but mortification can also be characteristic of Christian image repair. When image restoration discourse follows an accusation of wrongdoing that the accused recognizes as a violation of their religious principles or convictions, mortification is effective and consistent with antecedent rhetoric. Swaggart used mortification initially in his public apology. It was consistent with his religious tradition, and it likely would have worked to cleanse his image if he had not retreated from it and attempted to evade responsibility and reduce offensiveness. If religious rhetorical tradition and biblical authority influence their choices, then it would be appropriate for Christian rhetors to heed the suggestion in I John 1:9, "If we confess our sins, he is faithful and just and will forgive us our sins and purify us from all unrighteousness." In addition, corrective action might be a meaningful companion to mortification as a means of providing restoration to a situation.

As was shown in several cases, bolstering and attacking accusers can be useful and unique as strategies in a Christian *apologia*. Notably, Paul and Justin used bolstering to strengthen their individual credibility and the ethos of the sect. Attacks were used in nearly every case as an instrument for marking boundaries between themselves and their opponents.

It would, perhaps, be less appropriate for Christian apologists to frequently use tactics designed to evade responsibility. According to Christian tradition, if an individual is wrong, he/she should admit it and be restored. If he/she is not wrong, it would be unnecessary to avoid responsibility. Swaggart demonstrates the folly of not fully carrying out such mortification in the face of obvious wrongdoing.

Audience and Evaluation

These cases of *apologia* operated somewhat differently than political, corporate, and celebrity image restoration in that the salient audiences were not as clearly defined and determined. While Paul's primary audience was the Galatians, Justin's was the political leaders, Luther's was largely the German people, Swaggart's was his viewers and financial supporters, the Jesus Seminar opponents' was the spiritually inquisitive public, and the Southern Baptists' was made up of supporters and the general public, there seemed to be another auditing presence with which these apologists were concerned. Christian apologists seem to be concerned with God and their particular religious traditions as salient audiences. This would account for Jesus accepting his crucifixion and still being declared successful (Blaney & Benoit, 1997); Justin being martyred, yet having such a profound impact on church rhetoric; and Luther being championed as a victor in the face of excommunication. This ever-present audience in Christian *apologia* has a significant effect on the assessment of rhetorical effectiveness.

The presence of God as an audience, the influence of antecedent religious constraints, and transcendent epistemology all have an impact on determining the rhetorical effectiveness of Christian *apologia*. Since religious apologists are not primarily motivated by voters, stockholders, customers, or fans, their discourse can be treated differently.

If critics judge the effectiveness of image repair efforts by pragmatic, external impacts, then religious apologists like Jesus, Paul, Justin, and Luther would be failures because they suffered publicly as a result of the accusations brought against them. However, martyrs and exiles often take places in history as successful rhetors.

A strong transcendent appeal that is consistent with antecedent genres, and that positions "God as my witness," can result in a self-referential *apologia*. Using the criteria of God as audience, biblical and church history as reference, and transcendent epistemology as guide, it would be conceivable for apologists to suffer immense social failure, yet still declare themselves successful. If the use of transcendence positions a new cosmic standard for truth, then no amount of temporal failure can doom the apology. While this approach may provide solace for apologists who must suffer greatly for their actions, whose defenses are not sufficient to cleanse them of public guilt, it is problematic as a justification for the self-righteous who spurn the opinions of their various publics. This problem may account for the fact that some of the apologists in this study constructed generally consistent strategies, but failed to adequately persuade their audiences. Religious apologists need to be cognizant of this potential weakness in their discourse and should seek to be successful by maintaining a consistency with the accepted expectations of their religious tradition and epistemology. However, if they desire to actually purify their public image, they should not neglect the expectations of other audiences.

It would be inaccurate, or at least premature, to say that I have characterized *religious apologia*; more work would need to expand these preliminary interpretations to other faiths. It is not even entirely fair to say that what is described here is a *Christian apologia*, since there are so many denominations and cultural variations within Christianity that are not represented. So for now I will label it as protestantic Christian *apologia*: an image restoration discourse performed by Christian figures who may not represent Protestantism, but who, by their rhetoric, find a place within a protestant lineage. These protestantic figures champion such issues as salvation by grace, the authority of scripture, and autonomy of the individual.

Analysis of these Christian apologists reveals five distinct rhetorical traits. First, they are profoundly influenced by antecedent constraints, with a great deal of attention given to the precedents from the Bible and church history. Second, the most important image restoration strategies for them are transcendence and mortification, with some usefulness found in denying offensiveness, bolstering credibility, and attacking their accusers. Third, they are more likely than other public figures to engage in apologies that are prompted by epistemological conflicts. Fourth, they regularly define God, explicitly or operationally, as a salient audience for their apology. Last, they are often unconcerned about the approval of their immediate auditors, which can promote a self-referential (self-righteous) form of discourse.

CHRISTIAN RHETORIC

I would like to connect these discoveries with some current thinking on the nature of religious rhetoric. It is not my intention to construct a complete theory of religious rhetoric here; that would invoke an infinitely frustrating dispute over culture, linguistics, hermeneutics, theology, epistemology, religious practices, and denominational territoriality; therefore, I will simply briefly discuss how my findings contribute to the ongoing discussions on the subject.

It is sensible to begin with the life and rhetoric of Christ to locate defining characteristics of a Christian rhetoric (see Hobbs, 1998). Berry (1998) agrees with this assessment and submits that two characteristics of a Christian rhetoric would be paradox and pardon. The notion of paradox grows out of Jesus' seemingly counterintuitive teachings that suggested victory came from loss, strength from weakness, justice from mercy, life from death, etc. In an essay concerning religious metaphor, Miller (1999a) advances this idea by exploring the image of "Jesus as scandalon" as a critical part of Christian rhetorical epistemology. Referencing Kierkegaard and Bakhtin, McCracken (1994) suggests that the implicit paradox of the Gospels scandalizes, or offends the unbeliever's way of thinking; individuals are left with the choices of offense or faith.

The concept of pardon is rooted in the message of grace and hope rather than condemnation and punishment. Jesus' acts of love, as recorded in the Gospels and the rest of the New Testament, reveal a concern for others and a profound interest in the purification and transformation of individuals. Countless Christian authors such as Thomas Merton and C. S. Lewis designate grace, or the idea of unmerited favor, as a defining characteristic of Christian faith.

Perhaps another feature of Christian rhetoric is reconciliation. For instance, in the cases considered above, there seems to be more at stake than just the restoration of a public image; often the desire seems to be a reconciling of relationships. Christian *apologia*, as face-saving discourse, seems to primarily focus on either transcending (and by so doing, transforming) the standards of "the world" (Romans 12:2) and *reflecting* the face of God, or "mortifying the flesh" (Romans 8:13; Colossians 3:5) and *turning to* the face of God. In either case, the end motive is not to turn attention back to self, or, strictly speaking, to restore the face of the rhetor. Sullivan (1998b) clarifies this facial relationship when he writes:

As God's face in the world, we presence Him. We dwell in the shadow of the almighty—He is our habitation, our ethos. Living in that ethos, we are imbued with His Spirit and exhibit the fruit of His Spirit, our manifest ethos. We are motivated by His love and by our sensitivity to others; this is our pathos. We bring the message of reconciliation, that God has reconciled the world to himself, our logos. (p. 4)

If, in all cases, Christian believers reflect the face of God through Christ, then it seems inevitable that what passes as Christian rhetoric should reconcile relationships, or create peace, by either transcending or mortifying in this function.

In transcending the accepted reality of audiences, Christian discourse will likely become paradoxical, if not at least enigmatic in its nature. Mortification will likely accent the pardon found in grace. By working to reconcile relationships, rather than simply restoring damaged reputations, peace will be promoted. Therefore, the characteristics of paradox, pardon, and peace seem to be appropriate as a preliminary description of Christian rhetoric.

This approach to Christian rhetoric, by avoiding a moral tone that designates God-terms, devil-terms, and narrowly defined precepts as the parameters of a Christian rhetoric, avoids "establishing orthodoxy or reifying schisms" (Sullivan, 1998b, p. 4). Therefore, this approach provides for many voices to be heard in forming an understanding of what it means to say that discourse is uniquely Christian. It opens the way for a perspectival approach to religious rhetoric (see Miller, 1999a) that preserves the nature of core Christian beliefs without dictating specific beliefs and practices.

CONCLUSION

In closing this chapter I suggest some implications and limitations of this study. First, these cases were wide in scope and comprehensive in many fashions, but they do not represent the totality of Christian *apologia*. They were useful in illustrating the various ways faith-based image restoration is carried out, but future research should expand in content and method. To build a thorough foundation for Christian *apologia*, a comprehensive analysis should be done of all New Testament defenses. This would serve as an epistemic ground zero for further discussions. After that preliminary work is complete, it would be meaningful to extend the research beyond rhetoric that is so often dominated by voices that are Protestant,

Western, and male. Beyond these broad strokes, future studies could look at other second-century martyrs, Reformation leaders, televangelist scandals, scholarly disputes, denominational squabbles, or differences in Catholic, Orthodox, and Protestant *apologia*. Additionally, topics could be narrowed to such things as a treatment of Southern Baptist *apologia* on issues such as convention fights, apologies for support of slavery, public conflict over homosexuality issues, and the recent crisis the SBC faced after it aggressively targeted Jews for conversion.

Second, this project could serve as a preliminary work in the formation of a more general approach to religious *apologia* and rhetoric. Studies could examine the discourse of other faith traditions, taking on the discourses of Judaism, Islam, and Buddhism, for instance, with an aim toward creating a taxonomy of image restoration strategies and rhetorical characteristics that are common to all religious rhetors.

Some of the limitations that studies of religious *apologia* will always face are locating audiences and using sacred texts as artifacts. With such a transcendent tone at work in their discourse, it is often difficult to determine at which audience the discourse is aimed. Was Paul always addressing the Galatians, or was he communicating with the Jewish leadership? Was Luther interested in convincing the Diet of Worms, or did he just want to persuade the German people? Were the Southern Baptist apologists talking to those within their denomination, or the public as a whole? These questions are difficult to answer and, therefore, the specific evaluation of rhetorical success is decidedly imprecise. The same lack of clarity is inherent in using biblical texts as rhetorical examples. It could be viewed as tautological that Paul's discourse in Galatians is successful. Paul's letter may likely have been chosen for inclusion in the New Testament canon *because* it was successful. In fact, many of the documents included in scripture likely represent the more successful cases of Hebrew and Christian rhetoric, and are, therefore, successful from the outset.

Finally, any study of religious *apologia* must come to terms with the unique epistemological challenges faced by the rhetors. Epistemological issues are of great importance in understanding the nature of religious image restoration discourse. Political, corporate, and celebrity image repair generally concern such pragmatic issues as re-election, quarterly profits, or commercial marketability; religious *apologia* is distinct in that it is uniquely involved in the matters of the soul. Certainly other material concerns intervene, but for the most part the manner in which individuals come to know has a great deal of impact on their ethical character. Wood (1998) submits that epistemology is not just about the process of knowledge; it involves dimensions of intellectual virtue. Therefore, epistemological issues as they relate to image should be of serious concern to the Christian apologist and critic.

Regardless of the limitations of this, or any future study of religious discourse, this project contributes a significant expansion of the theory of image restoration discourse, and it offers a new theoretical approach to the specific practice of Christian *apologia*. In general, I found that Christian *apologia* is quite different from other forms of image restoration. It employs a distinct group of strategies, marked by the distinct influence of transcendence.

8

Implications for Image Restoration Discourse

As a way of articulating this study's contribution to the theory of image restoration discourse, I will first consider the appropriateness of Benoit's model, giving special attention to specific image repair strategies. I will further examine the book's contribution to an understanding of group *apologia*. And I will discuss the role of epistemology in image restoration. This section will conclude by addressing some limitations of image restoration theory, and some possible modifications.

USEFULNESS OF IMAGE RESTORATION THEORY

This study demonstrates that Benoit's theory of image restoration discourse is appropriate and useful for analyzing religious *apologia*. The distinct context of faith-based defenses served to refine some of the components of Benoit's theory. For instance, when the theory of image restoration discourse begins by claiming that individuals and groups are fundamentally motivated to preserve their image, these cases demonstrated that some religious apologists may be entirely unconcerned about personal face issues, yet they associate their beliefs (policies) with their character and, therefore, they are significantly motivated to restore any damage to the credibility of those beliefs.

Furthermore, Benoit's typology provides a comprehensive schema by which to understand any form of self-defense rhetoric, even uniquely Christian rhetoric. Religious texts are replete with examples of people who, when faced with accusations, either deny, make excuses (evade responsibility), justify their behavior (reduce offensiveness), or seek forgiveness and restoration (mortification and corrective action). There appear to be no other discursive options available to rhetors, religious or not. Therefore, image restoration theory has been shown meaningful as a means of conceptualizing religious self-defense discourse.

Development of Strategies

The most significant development in image restoration strategies in this study is a broadening of transcendence. Up until this point, transcendence has been viewed as an appeal to some higher value or context (see Benoit, 1995a), or as a claim that the accusations are a distraction from matters of greater importance (Benoit & Wells, 1998; Blaney, 1998). While these are accurate and useful observations about transcendence, this study suggests that transcendence performs another function: It advocates a competing perspective on reality.

When the apologists in this study transcended, often they were not simply broadening the scope of the issue or advocating a return to important matters, they were suggesting an entirely new worldview. For example, Paul was not only arguing that grace was a higher spiritual value or a matter of greater importance, he was advocating a revolutionary change in the criteria for offensiveness. He maintained that the "truth" had changed and that people no longer achieved righteousness through the law, but received it as a gift. Likewise, when the traditionalist apologists transcended in their responses to the Jesus Seminar, they were objecting to a naturalistic standard for truth. By advocating a competing form of truth, they were arguing that what their accusers viewed as offensive was, in fact, not offensive because their criteria for offensiveness were flawed.

While this dimension of transcendence may seem like a relatively insignificant variance from previously developed concepts of transcendence, it has a significant impact on how defenses are made. For example, if opposing rhetors view transcendence as simply a higher value or a more important matter, they face the potential of rejecting the higher value or important matter and returning to their shared reality. However, if the basis of the transcendence is divergent world-views, or *Weltenschauungen*, then there is little likelihood of ever returning to "business as usual." The nature of this transcendence may account for the seeming incommensurability of many religious believers and their opponents (i.e., creation/evolution, pro-life/pro-choice, biblical literalists/interpretivists, etc.).

This study also expands the strategy of denial. Where most previous research has described denial as either a simple rejection of the accusations or as shifting the blame, this study, along with Brinson and Benoit's (1996) study of Dow Corning, reveals another dimension. In many cases it seemed that apologists denied the offensiveness without actually denying the performance of the offensive act. Luther did not deny writing the books attributed to him; he simply denied that they were heretical, or offensive. Southern Baptist apologists did not deny passing the amendment to their faith statement; they just denied that it was offensive. This is a significant extension of denial, because previously it might have been considered inconsistent for an apologist to deny an offense and transcend the accusations in the same defense. If denials can be viewed as focusing only on the rejection of the offensiveness, then the apologist can make a consistent defense using transcendence with denial.

In addition to transcendence and denial, this study promotes a better understanding of the strategy of attacking accusers. It seems to be a less prominent strategy when the accusers are present during the defense, especially if the attackers are primary auditors for the discourse. Perhaps that is a conflict avoidance technique on the part of the apologist, but it stands to reason that a counterattack will probably have more impact if launched from a distance. In the case of Luther's defense, he avoided a direct attack against his accusers when he was standing before the Diet of Worms. While attacking accusers can serve an effective purpose for apologists, it would be best saved for defenses that do not involve face-to-face encounters with the accusers.

Another question raised by this study concerns the extent to which the accusers are the salient audience in a defense. Perhaps the relevant audiences are often a public distinct from the attackers, which would explain the use of attacks against accusers as a frequent rhetorical strategy. If the apologist is not particularly interested in the persuasive impact on his/her attackers, it would make sense to attack them.

Group *Apologia*

It is worthwhile to note the difference between a group *apologia* and surrogate defense. Benoit and Wells (1998) and Blaney (1998) describe surrogate defenses as image restoration discourse that is performed by an individual on behalf of another accused individual or group. The distinction between surrogates and group apologists is that a surrogate is not an object of the original accusation. Surrogates stand outside the attack as an advocate for the accused. Likewise, group apologists are not individually accountable for the charges; however, they are somehow associated with others in such a way that they, as a group, perceive the attacks to be against them and they share a collective motive to respond to accusations. For instance, in the two cases of group *apologia* in this study—the traditionalist apologists responding to the Jesus Seminar and the Southern Baptist representatives—the defenders treated the attacks against the groups as attacks against their personal images. So the traditionalists and the Southern Baptists were not operating as surrogates for their respective organizations or religious identities; they were responding as members of the collective accused.

There appeared to be little strategic difference in defenses made by a group of apologists and the apology of an individual. The traditionalist apologists and the Southern Baptists did not use any tactics that were particularly unique from those used by individual rhetors. In fact, in a comparison between the group apologists and Justin's defense of the group of early Christians, the only difference is the use of differentiation by the two contemporary cases. Unlike Paul, Luther, and Swaggart, Justin was primarily defending a group with which he was identified; however, his tactics were not markedly different from other individual defenses or the group defenses.

This seems to indicate that as a group establishes an identifiable image, and as individuals become enculturated in a group, the group takes on a public face that operates in much the same way as the public image of an individual. Therefore, the apologists for groups seem to respond in much the same way as if their own personal image was being assaulted.

Some Limitations and Modifications

In addition to the suggestions made above, I offer further comments on Benoit's theory of image restoration discourse as it relates to this project. First, I share the concerns of Burns and Bruner (2000)[1] about the term "image." I do not object to the use of the term, simply the implication that in all cases of image restoration there is a single image with which to be concerned. As detailed above, groups often are the sources of *apologia*, and "a [group's] image is not unitary nor homogeneous" (Burns & Bruner, p. 29). If we are not careful, it would be easy to begin to see a group's image as a totality that is seen as all bad or all good by all audiences. The fact is that all apologists, individual and corporate, contain and express a variety of images that need to be taken into account. This is not to say that our analysis should always attempt to include a potentially infinite number of images; however, we should be careful to avoid becoming unduly myopic in our investigations.

In a similar vein, I would agree with Burns and Bruner's criticism that Benoit's theory can promote "attack and image restoration as a two-step, linear or, at best, turn-taking process" (p. 30) that is unnecessarily reductionist. If image restoration theory portrays a static view of rhetoric as specific messages precisely designed to answer other specific messages, the whole rhetorical enterprise is reduced to a stimulus-response model. Fortunately, this is not the intent, or the effect, of the theory (see Benoit, 2000). In some cases it might be best to expand the notion of what the relevant "images" are, what multiplicity of goals and motives inhere in a message, and recognize that "restoration" as a completed condition is an unlikely result. However, there are other cases where "image repair does occur as a particular discursive response to a specific rhetorical attack" (Benoit, 2000, p. 41), requiring a relatively linear process of analysis. On the whole, this issue serves as a warning for scholars to allow ambiguity and flexibility in the process, rather than viewing the theory as a set of sacrosanct precepts and categories within which any defensive discourse can be stuffed.

Another concern with image restoration theory is the manner in which outcomes are assessed. Burns and Bruner express some doubts about the theory's ability to determine the effectiveness of an *apologia*. They agree with the appropriateness standards applied by Benoit and his colleagues. For instance, Kennedy and Benoit (1997) found that Newt Gingrich's defense of himself was inappropriate because he denied the accusations, then offered to take corrective action (for something he had denied doing). Burns and Bruner take exception, however, with the tendency to pronounce judgment on an *apologia* because of some perceived changes in the external world. The problem is in determining what the exact relationship is between the discourse and the subsequent events. Just because President Clinton's approval ratings rose after his transcendent rhetoric, that does not necessarily indicate a causal relationship. The public may have been expressing support for a policy change, with no interest in the *apologia*. This is a perennial problem faced by rhetorical critics that Benoit (2000) partially addresses by referring his critics to the standards proposed by Stromer-Galley and Schiappa (1998) for rigorous proof of effects. He also argues that critics must not ignore the evidence of effects that may not be absolutely causally connected. However, in the end, there will always be some question as to how direct the impact of an *apologia* is on external events.

It is difficult to determine what makes audiences react the way they do. It is possible that the various responses to the rhetors in this study were largely based on spiritual, cultural, or emotional responses to situations beyond the content of the discourse. For instance, when determining the effectiveness of the discourse we could take time into account. We are able to assess the rhetoric of Paul, Justin, and Luther over great expanses of time. The historical, religious, and cultural impacts are well-documented and available for consideration. However, the contemporary examples do not receive the same consideration. For example, it is conceivable that hundreds of years from now, Swaggart's defense may evolve and be seen as largely successful. If his fortune turns and he becomes widely successful again as a televangelist, the impact of his rhetoric will likely change in the historical scope of things. So evaluations of the success of image restoration discourse should take the effect of time into account. Questions remain as to whether the actual discourse affected the audiences in the manners assumed, or if there were other influences. This present study is incapable of making that determination. And perhaps that is as it should be. If rhetoric is indeed an art form, I contend that it is illegitimate to feel overly compelled to exhaustively assess its effectiveness. For the rhetorical practitioner who is primarily interested in proven strategies that will elicit certain responses, a rhetorical criticism is probably not the best place to look.

This leads to the final concern with the theory. Image restoration theory is very useful as a descriptive model, but it seems to promise little help in prescribing strategies for future rhetors. I believe that this is a current weakness in the theory, but one that will change as more research is conducted. As the opportunities for research expand, and the findings of image restoration studies continue to mount up,[2] there will be more opportunity to trace some trends as to which strategies work better in certain circumstances. This, however, does not address the capacity rhetors will always have to ineptly execute strategies, no matter how well they have worked for others in similar situations. This leads me back to a familiar point: Rhetoric is an art and human behavior will always be relatively unpredictable. Therefore, it is neither my intention, nor my desire, to supply a set of conditions under which a specifically prescribed set of strategies should be used. It is, however, my intention to present cases and my accompanying analysis, such as these above, as stimulants that might percolate through the minds of potential rhetors.

SUMMARY

I found Benoit's theory of image restoration discourse to be useful as an instrument for rhetorical criticism. This study expanded the application of the theory to the field of religion, which proved to be meaningful for a maturing of the theory and in advancing our understanding of the discourse of faith. While there are a few areas in which the theory still needs work, on the whole it has proven to be profoundly important as an advancement in human communication research.

NOTES

1. Burns and Bruner address a number of other issues with regard to Benoit's theory of image restoration discourse. Among the topics I have mentioned, they recommend expanding the frame of analysis to take in a broader scope of actions and reactions, promoting more of an audience perspective as an alternative to a source-orientation, recognizing the way in which postmodernity has fragmented texts and contexts, and considering structural factors beyond discourse that affect image repair. I chose not to address all of these here, since they were either beyond the scope of my inquiry, or Benoit (2000) has answered them sufficiently in his response.

2. Future researchers could follow the prompting of Craig (1999) and engage in a blended form of research across traditions. For instance, the theory of image restoration discourse could be combined with the sociopsychological approach of politeness theory to consider the possible strategies and measurable outcomes of doctor-patient interaction. Image

restoration could be blended with cultural or critical approaches to compare the apologetic discourse of Christian men in the Promise Keepers with their female counterparts in Heritage Keepers. Or image restoration could be blended with cybernetic methods to consider the nature of computer-mediated image repair.

Bibliography

Ammerman, N. T. (1990). *Baptist battles: Social change and religious conflict in the Southern Baptist Convention.* London: Rutgers University Press.

Aristotle. (1991). *On rhetoric.* (G. A. Kennedy, Trans.). New York: Oxford University Press.

Atkinson, J. (1971). *The trial of Luther.* New York: Stein and Day.

Bainton, R. H. (1950). *Here I stand: A life of Martin Luther.* New York: The New American Library.

Baptist faith and message (1963/1998) [Online]. Nashville, TN: Sunday School Board of the Southern Baptist Convention. Available: http://www.sbc.net/bfm.cfm.

Barnhart, J. E. (1986). *The Southern Baptist holy war.* Austin: Texas Monthly Press.

Baskerville, B. (1952). The vice-presidential candidates. *Quarterly Journal of Speech, 38,* 406–408.

Battista, B. (Host)(1998, June 10). The Southern Baptist Convention on the role of women in family. *CNN Talkback Live.* Washington, DC: Cable News Network.

Benoit, W. L. (1982). Richard M. Nixon's rhetorical strategies in his public statements on Watergate. *Southern Speech Communication Journal, 47,* 192–211.

Benoit, W. L. (1988). Senator Edward M. Kennedy and the Chappaquiddick tragedy. In H. R. Ryan (Ed.), *Oratorical encounters: Selected studies and sources of twentieth-century political accusations and apologies* (pp. 187–199). Westport, CT: Greenwood Press.

Benoit, W. L. (1995a). *Accounts, excuses, apologies: A theory of image restoration strategies.* Albany: State University of New York Press.

Benoit, W. L. (1995b). Sears' repair of its auto service image: Image restoration discourse in the corporate sector. *Communication Studies, 46,* 89–105.

Benoit, W. L. (1997a). Hugh Grant's image restoration discourse: An actor apologizes. *Communication Quarterly, 45,* 251–267.

Benoit, W. L. (1997b). Image repair discourse and crisis communication. *Public Relations Review, 23,* 177–187.

Benoit, W. L. (1999). Bill Clinton in the Starr chamber. *American Communication Journal, 3,* http://www.americancomm.org/~aca/acj/acj.html.

Benoit, W. L. (2000). Another visit to the theory of image restoration strategies. *Communication Quarterly, 48,* 40–44.

Benoit, W. L., & Anderson, K. K. (1996). Blending politics and entertainment: Dan Quayle versus Murphy Brown. *Southern Communication Journal, 62,* 73–85.

Benoit, W. L., & Brinson, S. (1994). AT&T: Apologies are not enough. *Communication Quarterly, 42,* 75–88.

Benoit, W. L., & Brinson, S. L. (1999). Queen Elizabeth's image repair discourse: Insensitive royal or compassionate Queen? *Public Relations Review, 25,* 145–156.

Benoit, W. L., & Czerwinski, A. (1997). A critical analysis of USAir's image repair discourse. *Business Communication Quarterly, 60,* 38–57.

Benoit, W. L., & Dorries, B. (1996). Dateline NBC's persuasive attack of Wal-Mart. *Communication Quarterly, 44,* 463–477.

Benoit, W. L., Gullifor, P., & Panici, D. (1991). President Reagan's defensive discourse on the Iran-Contra affair. *Communication Studies, 42,* 272–294.

Benoit, W. L., & Hanczor, R. (1994). The Tonya Harding controversy: An analysis of image repair strategies. *Communication Quarterly, 42,* 416–433.

Benoit, W. L., & Lindsey, J. J. (1987). Argument strategies: Antidote to Tylenol's poisoned image. *Journal of the American Forensic Association, 23,* 136–146.

Benoit, W. L., & Nill, D. M. (1998a). Oliver Stone's defense of JFK. *Communication Quarterly, 46,* 127–143.

Benoit, W. L., & Nill, D. M. (1998b). A critical analysis of Judge Clarence Thomas' statement before the Senate Judiciary Committee. *Communication Studies, 39,* 179–195.

Benoit, W. L., & Wells, W. T. (1998). An analysis of three image repair discourses on Whitewater. *Journal of Public Advocacy, 3*, 21–37.

Benson, J. A. (1988). Crisis revisited: An analysis of strategies used by Tylenol in the second tampering episode. *Central States Speech Journal, 39,* 49–66.

Berry, E. (1998). *A Christian rhetoric: Whose? To what end?* Paper presented at the National Communication Association Convention, New York.

Betz, H. D. (1979). *Galatians: A commentary on Paul's Letter to the Churches in Galatia.* Philadelphia: Fortress Press.

Blair, C. (1984). From *All the President's Men* to every man for himself: The strategies of post Watergate apologia. *Central States Speech Journal, 35,* 250–260.

Blaney, J. R., & Benoit, W. L. (1997). The persuasive defense of Jesus in the Gospel according to John. *Journal of Communication and Religion, 20,* 25–30.

Blaney, J. R., & Benoit, W. L. (2001). *The Clinton scandals and the politics of image restoration.* Westport, CT: Praeger.

Blomberg, C. L. (1994). The seventy-four "scholars": Who does the Jesus Seminar speak for? Christian Research Institute. Available at http://www.rim.org/muslim/jesusseminar.htm.

Blumhofer, E. (1987, May 6). Divided Pentecostals: Bakker vs. Swaggart. *The Christian Century, 104,* 430–431.

Blumhofer, E. (1988, April 6). Swaggart and the Pentecostal ethos. *The Christian Century, 105,* 333–335.

Bock, C. L. (1995). The words of Jesus in the Gospels: Live, jive, or Memorex? In M. F. Wilkins & F. P. Moreland (Eds.), *Jesus under fire: Modern scholarship reinvents the historical Jesus* (pp. 73–100). Grand Rapids, MI: Zondervan.

Borg, M. J. (1994). *Meeting Jesus again for the first time: The historical Jesus and the heart of contemporary faith.* San Francisco: HarperCollins.

Borg, M. J., & Wright, N. T. (1999). *The meaning of Jesus: Two visions.* San Francisco: HarperCollins.

Brinson, S., & Benoit, W. L. (1996). Dow Corning's image repair strategies in the breast implant crisis. *Communication Quarterly, 44,* 29–41.

Brinson, S., & Benoit, W. L. (1999). The tarnished star: Restoring Texaco's damaged public image. *Management Communication Quarterly, 12,* 483–510.

Brock, B. L. (1988). Gerald R. Ford encounters Richard Nixon's legacy: On amnesty and the pardon. In H. R. Ryan (Ed.), *Oratorical encounters: Selected studies and sources of twentieth-century political accusations and apologies* (pp. 227–240). Westport, CT: Greenwood Press.

Brockriede, W. (1974). Rhetorical criticism as argument. *Quarterly Journal of Speech, 60,* 166 174.

Bruce, F. F. (1982). *The Epistle to the Galatians: A commentary on the Greek text.* Grand Rapids, MI: Eerdmans Publishing.

Brummett, B. (1975). Presidential substance: The address of August 15, 1973. *Western Speech Communication, 39,* 249–259.

Bultmann, R. (1934). *Jesus and the word.* New York: Scribner's.

Burke, K. (1970). *The rhetoric of religion.* Berkeley: University of California Press.

Burns, J. P., & Bruner, M. S. (2000). Revisiting the theory of image restoration strategies. *Communication Quarterly, 48,* 27–39.

Butler, S. D. (1972). The *apologia:* 1971 genre. *Southern Speech Communication Journal, 36,* 281–290.

Carlson, M. (1998, September 14). Now say it like you mean it: Clinton was once the master of the apology act, so why can't he fake it again? *Time, 152,* 44.

Carnell, E. J. (1956). *An introduction to Christian apologetics.* Grand Rapids, MI: Eerdmans Publishing.

Clark, D. K. (1993). *Dialogical apologetics: A person-centered approach to Christian defense.* Grand Rapids, MI: Baker.

Clark, R. A., & Delia, R. J. (1979). *Topoi* and rhetorical competence. *Quarterly Journal of Speech, 65,* 187–206.

Clash between the historical Jesus and spiritual Jesus. (1996, April 7). *ABC News.* New York: American Broadcasting Companies.

Clinton disagrees. (1998, June 11). *Pittsburgh Post-Gazette,* p. A9.

Collins, A. A., & Clark, J. E. (1992). Jim Wright's resignation speech: Delegitimization or redemption? *Southern Communication Journal, 58,* 67–75.

Craig, W. L. (1995). Did Jesus rise from the dead? In M. F. Wilkins & F. P. Moreland (Eds.), *Jesus under fire: Modern scholarship reinvents the historical Jesus* (pp. 141–176). Grand Rapids, MI: Zondervan.

Crossan, J. D. (1991). *The historical Jesus: The life of a Mediterranean Jewish peasant.* San Francisco: HarperCollins.

Crossan, J. D. (1995). *Who killed Jesus? Exposing the roots of anti-Semitism in the Gospel story of the death of Jesus.* San Francisco: HarperCollins.

Crossan, J. D. (Speaker) (1998, April 9). *Talk of the nation.* Washington, DC: National Public Radio.

Crownfield, F. R. (1945). The singular problem of the dual Galatians. *Journal of Biblical Literature, 63,* 491–500.

Dionisopoulos, G. N., & Vibbert, S. L. (1988). CBS vs. Mobil Oil: Charges of creative bookkeeping in 1979. In H. R. Ryan (Ed.), *Oratorical encounters: Selected studies and sources of twentieth-century political accusations and apologies* (pp. 241–251). Westport, CT: Greenwood Press.

Draper, J. T. (1984). *Authority: The critical issue for Southern Baptists.* Old Tappan, NJ: Fleming H. Revell.

Dulles, A. (1971). *A history of apologetics.* New York: Corpus.

Edwards, J. R. (1996). Who do scholars say that I am? *Christianity Today, 40,* 15–20.

Edwards, M. U. (1983). *Luther's last battles: Politics and polemics, 1531–46.* New York: Cornell University Press.

Edwards, M. U. (1990). *Lutherschmahung?* Catholics on Luther's responsibility for the Peasants' War. *Catholic Historical Review, 76,* 461–481.

Evans, C. S. (1996*). The historical Christ and the Jesus of faith: The incarnational narrative as history.* Oxford: Oxford University Press.

Farnsley, A. E. (1994). *Southern Baptist politics: Authority and power in the restructuring of an American denomination.* University Park: Pennsylvania State University.

Fisher, W. R. (1970). A motive view of communication. *Quarterly Journal of Speech, 56,* 131 139.

Foss, S. K. (1984). Retooling an image: Chrysler Corporation's rhetoric of redemption. *Western Journal of Speech Communication, 48,* 75–91.

Foxe, J. (1989). *Foxe's Christian martyrs of the world.* Uhrichsville, OH: Barbour Publishing. Originally published in 1559.

Frankl, R. (1987). *Televangelism: The marketing of popular religion.* Carbondale: Southern Illinois University Press.

Funk, R. W. (1985). The opening remarks of Jesus Seminar. *Forum, 01,* Available at http://www.westarinstitute.org/Jesus_Seminar/Remarks/remarks.html.

Funk, R. W. (1996). *Honest to Jesus: Jesus for a new millennium.* San Francisco: HarperCollins.

Funk, R. W. (Ed.) (1998). *The acts of Jesus: The search for the authentic deeds of Jesus.* New York: Macmillan.

Funk, R. W., Hoover, R. W., & the Jesus Seminar. (1993). *The five gospels: The search for the authentic words of Jesus.* New York: Macmillan.

Goffman, E. (1967). On face work. *Interaction ritual: Essays in face-to-face behavior* (pp. 5–45). Chicago: Aldine.

Gold, E. R. (1978). Political apologia: The ritual of self-defense. *Communication Monographs, 46,* 306–316.

Grant, R. M. (1988). *Greek apologists of the second century.* Philadelphia: Westminster Press.

Griffith, M., & Harvey, P. (1998). Wifely submission: The SBC resolution. *Christian Century, 115,* 636–638.

Gring, M. A. (1998). *Rhetoric as covenantal: Toward a theory of Christian rhetoric*. Paper presented at the National Communication Association Convention, New York.

Grossman, C. L. (1998, June 11). Baptists explain the moral tone. *USA Today*, p. 6D.

Haapanen, L. W. (1988). Nikita S. Khrushchev vs. Dwight D. Eisenhower. In H. R. Ryan (Ed.), *Oratorical encounters: Selected studies and sources of twentieth-century political accusations and apologies* (pp. 137–152). Westport, CT: Greenwood Press.

Habermas, G. R. (1995). Did Jesus perform miracles? In M. F. Wilkins, & F. P. Moreland (Eds.), *Jesus under fire: Modern scholarship reinvents the historical Jesus* (pp. 117–140). Grand Rapids, MI: Zondervan.

Hackett, G. (1988, February 29). A sex scandal breaks over Jimmy Swaggart. *Newsweek, 111*, 30–31.

Hadden, J. K., & Swann, C. E. (1981). *Prime time preachers: The rising power of televangelism.* Reading, MA: Addison-Wesley Publishing Company.

Harrell, J., Ware, B. L., & Linkugel, W. A. (1975). Failure of apology in American politics: Nixon on Watergate. *Speech Monographs, 42,* 245–261.

Hearit, K. M. (1995). "Mistakes were made": Organizations, apologia, and crises of social legitimacy. *Communication Studies, 46,* 1–17.

Hearit, K. M. (1996). The use of counter-attack in apologetic public relations crises: The case of General Motors vs. Dateline NBC. *Public Relations Review, 22,* 233–248.

Hearit, K. M. (1997). On the use of transcendence as an apologia strategy: The case of Johnson Controls and its fetal protection policy. *Public Relations Review, 23,* 217–232.

Heinemann, R. L. (1997). Secular spirituality and the evangelical search for rhetorical ground. *Journal of Communication and Religion, 20,* 53–65.

Heisey, D. R. (1988). President Ronald Reagan's apologia on the Iran-Contra affair. In H. R. Ryan (Ed.), *Oratorical encounters: Selected studies and sources of twentieth-century political accusations and apologies* (pp. 281–306). Westport, CT: Greenwood Press.

Heisey, D. R. (1998). Reflections on religious speech communication. *Journal of Communication and Religion, 21,* 85–107.

Hendrix, S. H. (1981). *Luther and the papacy: Stages in a Reformation conflict.* Philadelphia: Fortress Press.

Hester, J. D. (1984). The rhetorical structure of Galatians 1:11–14. *Journal of Biblical Literature, 103,* 223–233.

Hinson, E. G. (1996). *The early church: Origins to the dawn of the Middle Ages.* Nashville, TN: Abingdon Press.

Hobbs, J. D. (1998). *Christian rhetorical criticism: An extension and application.* Paper presented at the National Communication Association Convention, New York.

Howard, G. (1979). *Paul: Crisis in Galatia.* Cambridge: Cambridge University Press.

Huebner, T. M. (1991). A house divided: Heresy and orthodoxy in the Southern Baptist Convention. *Journal of Communication and Religion, 14,* 34–43.

Huxman S. S., & Linkugel, W. A. (1988). Accusations and apologies from a general, a senator, and a priest. In H. R. Ryan (Ed.), *Oratorical encounters: Selected studies and sources of twentieth-century political accusations and apologies* (pp. 29–52). Westport, CT: Greenwood Press.

Ice, R. (1991). Corporate publics and rhetorical strategies. *Management Communication Quarterly, 4,* 341–362.

Jackson, J. H. (1956). Clarence Darrow's "Plea in defense of himself." *Western Speech, 20,* 185–195.

Jamieson, K. H. (1973a). Antecedent genre as rhetorical constraint. *Philosophy and Rhetoric, 6,* 406–415.

Jamieson, K. H. (1973b). Generic constraints and the rhetorical situation. *Philosophy and Rhetoric, 6,* 162–170.

Jensen, D. (1973). *Confrontation at Worms: Martin Luther and the Diet of Worms.* Provo, UT: Brigham Young University Press.

Jensen, R. J. (1988). The media and the Catholic Church vs. Geraldine Ferraro. In H. R. Ryan (Ed.), *Oratorical encounters: Selected studies and sources of twentieth-century political accusations and apologies* (pp. 253–266). Westport, CT: Greenwood Press.

Jewett, R. (1971). The agitators and the Galatian congregation. *New Testament Studies, 17,* 198–212.

Jimmy Swaggart just says no. (1988, April 11). *U.S. News & World Report, 104,* 12–13.

Johnson, L. T. (1996). *The real Jesus: The misguided quest for the historical Jesus and the truth of the traditional Gospels.* San Francisco: HarperCollins.

Justin Martyr. (1907a). *Dialogue with Trypho, a Jew.* In A. Roberts & J. Donaldson (Eds.), *The Ante-Nicene Fathers* (pp. 194–270). Grand Rapids, MI: Eerdmans Publishing.

Justin Martyr. (1907b). *The First Apology.* In A. Roberts & J. Donaldson (Eds.), *The Ante-Nicene Fathers* (pp. 159–187). Grand Rapids, MI: Eerdmans Publishing.

Justin Martyr. (1907c). *The Second Apology.* In A. Roberts & J. Donaldson (Eds.), *The Ante Nicene Fathers* (pp. 188–193). Grand Rapids, MI: Eerdmans Publishing.

Kahl, M. (1984). *Blind Ambition* culminates in *Lost Honor*: A comparative analysis of John Dean's apologetic strategies. *Central States Speech Journal, 35,* 239–250.

Katula, R. (1975). The apology of Richard M. Nixon. *Today's Speech, 23,* 1–6.

Kennedy, G. A. (1980). *Classical rhetoric and its Christian and secular tradition from ancient to modern times* (2nd ed.). Chapel Hill: University of North Carolina Press.

Kennedy, G. A. (1984). *New Testament interpretation through rhetorical criticism.* Chapel Hill: University of North Carolina Press.

Kennedy, K. A., & Benoit, W. L. (1997). The Newt Gingrich book deal controversy: A case study in self-defense rhetoric. *Southern Communication Journal, 63,* 197–216.

King, L. (Host) (1998, June 12). Religion and family: The Southern Baptist Convention's view of marriage. *Larry King Live.* Washington, DC: Cable News Network.

King, W. (1988, February 23). Church orders 2-year rehabilitation for Swaggart. *New York Times.* A18.

King, W. (1988, February 24). Swaggart action relatively light. *New York Times.* A12.

Kittelson, J. M. (1992). The accidental revolutionary. *Christian History, 11,* 9–18.

Kloehn, S. (1998, June 10). Southern Baptists approve submissive wives doctrine. *Chicago Tribune,* p. 1N.

Klope, D. C. (1998). *No: Reflections on an oxymoron.* Paper presented at the National Communication Association Convention, New York.

Koukl, G. (1995). The Jesus Seminar under fire. *Stand to Reason* (radio program). Available at http://www.str.org/free/commentaries/apologetics/bible/jsuf.htm.

Kruse, N. W. (1977). Motivational factors in non-denial apologia. *Central States Speech Journal, 28,* 13–23.

Kruse, N. W. (1981a). *Apologia* in team sport. *Quarterly Journal of Speech, 67,* 270–283.

Kruse, N. W. (1981b). The scope of apologetic discourse: Establishing generic parameters. *Southern Speech Communication Journal, 46,* 278–291.

Kurtz, L. R. (1986). *The politics of heresy.* Berkeley: University of California Press.

Levy, L. W. (1993). *Blasphemy: Verbal offense against the sacred, from Moses to Salman Rushdie.* New York: Knopf.

Ling, D. A. (1970). A pentadic analysis of Senator Edward Kennedy's Address to the People of Massachusetts, July 25, 1969. *Central States Speech Journal, 21,* 81–86.

Lipscomb, S. (Producer/Director). (1996). *The battle for the minds* [Film]. Hohokus, NJ: New Day Films.

Luther, M. (1949). *Commentary on the Epistle to the Galatians* (T. Graebner, Trans.). Grand Rapids, MI: Zondervan. Originally published in 1535.

MacKinnon, J. (1962). *Luther and the Reformation: Vol. 2. The breach with Rome (1517–21)*. New York: Russell & Russell.

Marshall, P., & Gilbert, L. (1997). *Their blood cries out: The untold story of persecution against Christians in the modern world*. Nashville, TN: Word.

McCracken, D. (1994). *The scandal of the Gospels: Jesus, story, and offense*. New York: Oxford University Press.

McKnight, S. (1995). Who is Jesus? An introduction to Jesus studies. In M. F. Wilkins & F. P. Moreland (Eds.), *Jesus under fire: Modern scholarship reinvents the historical Jesus* (pp. 51–72). Grand Rapids, MI: Zondervan.

McLennan, D. B. (1996). Rhetoric and the legitimation process: The rebirth of Charles Colson. *Journal of Communication and Religion, 19,* 5–12.

Meeks, W. A. (Ed.). (1972). *The writings of St. Paul*. New York: W.W. Norton.

Meier, J. P. (1991). *A marginal Jew: Rethinking the historical Jesus* (Vol. 1). New York: Doubleday.

Mellowes, M. (1998, April 6). From Jesus to Christ: The first Christians. *Frontline*. New York: Public Broadcasting Service.

Miller, B. A. (1999a). Seeing through a glass darkly: Religious metaphor as rhetorical perspective. *Journal of Communication and Religion, 22,* 214–336.

Miller, B. A. (1999b). *A simple twist of faith: Spiritual ambiguity and rhetorical perspectivism in the music of Bob Dylan*. Paper presented at the National Communication Association Convention, Chicago.

Miller, B. A. (1999c). *Politeness theory and image restoration discourse within a metadiscursive model of communication*. Paper presented at the National Communication Association Convention, Chicago.

Neary, L. (Host) (1998, April 9). *Talk of the nation*. Washington, DC: National Public Radio.

Nelson, J. (1984). The defense of Billie Jean King. *Western Journal of Speech Communication, 48,* 92–102.

Olivier, D. (1978). *The trial of Luther*. London: Mowbrays.

Ostling, R. N. (1988a, March 7). Now it's Jimmy's turn. *Time, 131,* 46–48.

Ostling, R. N. (1988b, April 11). Worshipers on a holy roll. *Time, 131,* 55.

Phillips, J. B. (1955). *Letters to young churches*. New York: Macmillan.

Pomerantz, A. (1987). Attributions of responsibility: Blamings. *Sociology, 12,* 266–274.

Preachers who cast stones. (1988, February 29). *Time, 131,* 49.

Pullum, S. J. (1990). Accounting for the mass appeal of Jimmy Swaggart: Pentecostal media star. *Journal of Communication and Religion, 13,* 39–54.

Ramm, B. (1961). *Varieties of Christian apologetics.* Grand Rapids, MI: Baker Book House.

Reagles, S. L. (1998). *Christian theorizing on rhetoric: Heteroglossic variations on "Res" and "Verba" in contemporary homiletic texts.* Paper presented at the National Communication Association Convention, New York.

Report of committee on Baptist faith and message (1998) [online]. Available at: http://www.sbc.net/bfmreport1998.cfm.

Roberts, A., & Donaldson, J. (Eds.) (1907). *The Ante-Nicene fathers.* Grand Rapids, MI: Eerdmans Publishing.

Robinson, J. M. (1959). *A new quest for the historical Jesus.* Naperville, IL: A.R. Allenson.

Ropes, J. H. (1929). *The singular problem of the Epistle to the Galatians.* Cambridge: Harvard University Press.

Rosellini, L. (1988, March 7). Of rolexes and repentance. *U.S. News & World Report, 104,* 62–63.

Rosenfield, L. W. (1968). A case study in speech criticism: The Nixon-Truman analog. *Speech Monographs, 35,* 435–450.

Rourke, M. (1994, February 24). Who do people say I am? *Los Angeles Times,* p. E6.

Ryan, H. R. (1982). *Kategoria* and *apologia*: On their rhetorical criticism as a speech set. *Quarterly Journal of Speech, 68,* 254–261.

Ryan, H. R. (1988). Senator Richard M. Nixon's apology for "The fund." In H. R. Ryan (Ed.), *Oratorical encounters: Selected studies and sources of twentieth-century political accusations and apologies* (pp. 99–120). Westport, CT: Greenwood Press.

Ryan, H. R. (Ed.) (1988). *Oratorical encounters: Selected studies and sources of twentieth-century political accusations and apologies.* Westport, CT: Greenwood Press.

Scanlon, L. (1998, June 10). Southern Baptists urge wives to "submit" to spouses. *Courier Journal* (Louisville, KY), p. A1.

Schmithals, W. (1972). *Paul and the Gnostics.* (J. E. Steely, Trans.). Nashville, TN: Abingdon Press.

Schonbach, P. (1980). A category system for account phases. *European Journal of Social Psychology, 10,* 195–200.

Schultze, Q. J. (1991). *Televangelism and American culture: The business of popular religion.* Grand Rapids, MI: Baker.

Schweitzer, A. (1968). *The quest for the historical Jesus: A critical study of its progress from Reimarus to Wrede* (Revised edition). New York: Macmillan.

Schwiebert, E. G. (1950). *Luther and his times: The Reformation from a new perspective.* St. Louis: Concordia Publishing.

Scott, L. (1942). When Luther argued. *Quarterly Journal of Speech, 28,* 19–23.

Scott, M. H., & Lyman, S. M. (1968). Accounts. *American Sociological Review, 33,* 46–62.

Sellnow, T. L., & Ulmer, R. R. (1995). Ambiguous argument as advocacy in organizational crisis communication. *Argumentation and Advocacy, 31,* 138–150.

Sellnow, T. L., Ulmer, R. R., & Snider, M. (1998). The compatibility of corrective action in organizational crisis communication. *Communication Quarterly, 46,* 60–74.

Sheler, J. L., Tharp, M., & Seider, J. J. (1996, April 8). In search of Jesus. *U.S. News & World Report* [online], *120.* Available on LexisNexis.

Simon, E. (1968). *Luther alive: Martin Luther and the making of the Reformation.* Garden City, NY: Doubleday & Company.

Sproul, R. C., Gerstner, J., & Lindsley, A. (1984). *Classical apologetics: A rational defense of the Christian faith and a critique of presuppositional apologetics.* Grand Rapids, MI: Academie Books.

Steinfels, P. (1998, June 13). Beliefs. *New York Times,* p. A11.

Stone, W. S. (1992). The Southern Baptist controversy: A social drama. *Journal of Communication and Religion, 15,* 99–115.

Sullivan, D. L. (1998a). Francis Shaeffer's apparent apology in *Pollution and the Death of Man. Journal of Communication and Religion, 21,* 200–229.

Sullivan, D. L. (1998b). *Till we have faces: Exploring the issues, possibilities, and dangers of a Christian theory of rhetoric.* Paper presented at the National Communication Association Convention, New York.

Swaggart agonistes. (1988, February 27). *The Economist, 306,* 20–21.

Swaggart defies church leaders. (1988, March 31). *New York Times,* A18.

Swaggart goes it alone. (1988, April 18). *Time, 131,* 33.

Swaggart is barred from pulpit for one year. (1988, March 30). *New York Times,* p. A1.

Swaggart, J. (1988a, March). The Lord of breaking through. *The Evangelist,* pp. 4–9.

Swaggart, J. (1988b, April). I just want to say, "We love you." *The Evangelist,* p. 12.

Swaggart, J. (1988c, May). Following Jesus. *The Evangelist,* pp. 4–8.

Swaggart, J. (1988d, June). Blessed is the man . . . who passing through the Valley of Baca makes it a well. *The Evangelist,* pp. 4–12.

Swaggart, J. (1988e, August). Sixteen months out of the will of God. *The Evangelist,* pp. 4–10.

Swaggart, J. (1988f, December). Spiritual warfare. *The Evangelist,* pp. 4–12.

Swaggart, J. (1989, February). Evangelism. *The Evangelist*, pp. 4–9.

Swaggart, J. (1990, April). A hired servant. *The Evangelist*, pp. 3–7.

Taaffe, T. P. (1966). *The writings of the early church fathers*. New York: Monarch Press.

Toalston, A. (1998, July 27). 150-plus evangelicals underscore SBC marriage stance as biblical. *Baptist Press* [Online Press Release]. Available at: http://www.youareright.org/press_release.htm.

Tyler, L. (1997). Liability means never being able to say you're sorry: Corporate guilt, legal constraints, and defensiveness in corporate communication. *Management Communication Quarterly, 11*, 51–73.

Van Biema, D., & Ostling, R. N. (1996, April). The gospel truth? *Time, 147*, 52–57.

Vara, R., & Holmes, C. S. (1998, June 10). Baptists stand by the man. *Houston Chronicle*, p. A1.

Vartabedian, R. A. (1985). From Checkers to Watergate: Richard Nixon and the art of contemporary apologia. *Speaker and Gavel, 22*, 52–61.

Ware, B. L., & Linkugel, W. A. (1973). They spoke in defense of themselves: On the generic criticism of apologia. *Quarterly Journal of Speech, 59*, 273–283.

Warner, M. (Host) (1998, June 10). A woman's place? *Newshour with Jim Lehrer* [online]. Washington, DC: Public Broadcasting Service. Available at: http: www.pbs.org/newshour/bb/religion/jan-june98/.

Weaver, R. M. (1970). Language is sermonic. In R. L. Johannesen, R. Strickland, & R. T. Eubanks (Eds.), *Language is sermonic: Richard M. Weaver on the nature of rhetoric* (pp. 201–226). Baton Rouge: Louisiana State University Press.

Wehmeyer, P., & Jennings, P. (1998, June 10). Husbands, wives, and Southern Baptists. *ABC News*. New York: American Broadcasting Companies.

Weiss, J. (1998, June 20). Wifely submission: Is the quarrel with St. Paul? *Dallas Morning News*, p. 1G.

Wenham, D. (1995). *Paul: Follower of Jesus or founder of Christianity?* Grand Rapids, MI: Eerdmans Publishing.

White, G. (1989, September 30). Christ was no "goody two shoes," says organizer of Jesus Seminar. *Atlanta Journal-Constitution*, p. B8.

Wilkins, M. J., & Moreland, J. P. (Eds.) (1995). *Jesus under fire: Modern scholarship reinvents the historical Jesus*. Grand Rapids, MI: Zondervan.

William, D. E., & Treadway, G. (1992). Exxon and the Valdez accident: A failure in crisis communication. *Communication Studies, 43*, 56–64.

Wilson, A. N. (1997). *Paul: The mind of the Apostle*. New York: W.W. Norton & Company.

Wilson, A. N. (1998, June 16). The Bible according to Baptists. *New York Times*, p. A31.

Witherington, B. (1995). *Conflict and community in Corinth: A socio-rhetorical commentary on 1 and 2 Corinthians*. Grand Rapids, MI: Eerdmans Publishing.

Witherington, B. (1997). *Jesus quest: The third search for the Jew of Nazareth* (2nd ed.). Downers Grove, IL: InterVarsity Press.

Witherington, B. (1998). *The Paul quest: The renewed search for the Jew of Tarsus*. Downers Grove, IL: InterVarsity Press.

Wolterstorff, N., & Plantinga, A. (Eds.) (1983). *Faith and rationality*. Notre Dame, IN: University of Notre Dame Press.

Wood, W. J. (1998). *Epistemology: Becoming intellectually virtuous*. Downers Grove, IL: InterVarsity Press.

Woodward, K. L. (1988, March 7). The wages of sin. *Newsweek, 111,* 51.

Woodward, K. L. (1996, April 8). Rethinking the resurrection. *Newsweek, 127,* 60–68.

Wright, N. T. (1996). *Jesus and the victory of God*. Minneapolis: Fortress.

Wright, N. T. (1997). *What Saint Paul really said*. Grand Rapids, MI: Eerdmans Publishing.

Yamauchi, E. M. (1995). Jesus outside the New Testament: What is the evidence? In M. F. Wilkins & F. P. Moreland (Eds.), *Jesus under fire: Modern scholarship reinvents the historical Jesus* (pp. 207–230). Grand Rapids, MI: Zondervan.

Index

About the Author

BRETT A. MILLER is an assistant professor in the Department of Communication at Southwest Baptist University.